PRAYING

THE

PRIESTLY
PRAYER

WARREN M. MARCUS

CHARISMA
HOUSE

Visit the author's website at WarrenMarcus.com.

Library of Congress Cataloging-in-Publication Data:
An application to register this book for cataloging has been submitted to the Library of Congress.
International Standard Book Number: 978-1-63641-004-3
E-book ISBN: 978-1-63641-005-0

Portions of this book were previously published by Charisma House as *The Priestly Prayer of the Blessing*, ISBN 978-1-62999-491-8, copyright © 2018.

21 22 23 24 25 — 9 8 7 6 5 4 3 2 1
Printed in the United States of America

I want to honor my wife, Donna;
my son, Joseph;
and my daughter, Tara,
for their prayers and support.

Special thanks go to my mentors:
Pastor James Tate, Sid Israel Roth,
and Rev. Rick Amato.

I dedicate this book in memory of
my Messianic Jewish mother, Pearl Marcus,
who went home to be with the Lord at the age of 104.

CONTENTS

SECTION V:
MAY YHWH BE GRACIOUS TO YOU

SECTION VI:
MAY YHWH LIFT HIS COUNTENANCE
UPON YOU

SECTION VII:
MAY YHWH GIVE YOU PEACE

SECTION VIII:
PRAYING THE PRIESTLY PRAYER

"G-D" AND THE MYSTERY OF THE DASH!

W HEN I WROTE my book *The Priestly Prayer of the Blessing*, I referred to God as G-D and YHWH. I was torn about using G-D versus God and YHWH. In addition, I struggled with the use of Yeshua (Jesus) and Ruach HaKodesh (Holy Spirit). My publisher and I wondered whether Christians would stumble over these Hebrew names. But I felt a strong leading to refer to God as G-D. We decided this note to explain the unusual reference would clear things up for readers. Since the book you now hold, *Praying the Priestly Prayer*, is a thirty-day devotional that derives from that original book, this same explanation applies.

Though I was born and raised in a Jewish home and then in 1974 received Yeshua as my Messiah and Lord, I don't normally spell God "G-D." I'm familiar with the fact that religious Jewish people are taught to respect and honor the one true G-D of Israel in this fashion.

One key reason is this spelling refers to the tetragrammaton, a depiction in Hebrew of the sacred name of the one true G-D of Israel, which He gave to Moses in the Torah. The tetragrammaton contains only the consonants of G-D's sacred name and is expressed as Y-H-W-H. The vowels are missing, so the actual pronunciation of His sacred name is not fully known. Scholars can only speculate.

I am not asking anyone to refer this way to G-D, but I believe this is a teachable moment. This book takes the reader on a life-changing prayer journey with the heavenly Father as He makes Himself available to us in an intimate, supernatural, and experiential way! I believe the heavenly Father is about to make Himself known to the church like never before, and I believe this book is a tool He will use to help accomplish this purpose.

As you read this book, every time you see our heavenly Father referred to as G-D or YHWH, may it be a reminder that He seeks to reveal Himself to you in a new and deeper way. Like the hidden letters in the name, parts of our heavenly Father are waiting to be revealed as you seek a deeper, more intimate relationship with Him. It is not just knowing who our heavenly Father is. It is getting to know Him in the manner He always intended: intimately, supernaturally, and experientially!

PREFACE

WHAT IF THE one true G-D of Israel wrote a prayer that He wanted to be proclaimed over you every day? What if praying that prayer would bring supernatural favor, prosperity, abundance, healing, better relationships, protection, order, rest, wisdom, blessings, miracles, and so much more?

This supernatural prayer wouldn't be based on how good or perfect you are; it would be so powerful that through its daily proclamation over you, the one true G-D of Israel would give you the power to choose what is good and make godly decisions. The supernatural power of this prayer would propel you to be successful in all your endeavors.

The truth is, G-D did write such a prayer! The Jewish high priest Aaron chanted the prayer in Hebrew every day over the children of Israel when they were in the wilderness. It contains a very rich and deep impartation from our heavenly Father, and I am passionate about sharing it with you because I believe it can truly change your life.

I wrote a book titled *The Priestly Prayer of the Blessing*, found in Numbers 6:24–26, which explains the amazing benefits of this prayer and how I discovered the deep significance of the prayer's meaning. This book you now hold in your hands is a thirty-day journey that repurposes some of my first book's content into smaller, daily readings. The goal is to help you make this prayer and its blessings part of daily life both now and in the future.

Praying the Priestly Prayer has radically changed my life and what I experience every day by His power. I continually receive testimonies of believers who have experienced the supernatural power of praying the Priestly Prayer, and they see miracles happen regularly.

Let's begin this thirty-day journey to discover the blessings G-D has intended for us!

—WARREN M. MARCUS

SECTION I

THE POWER
OF THE
PRAYER

AN ANCIENT BLESSING AVAILABLE TODAY

The LORD bless you and keep you; the LORD make His face to shine
upon you, and be gracious unto you; the LORD lift His countenance upon
you, and give you peace.

—NUMBERS 6:24–26

ICALL THE PRAYER of blessing in Numbers 6:24–26 the Priestly Prayer of the Blessing. I wrote an entire book to reveal this prayer's significance. In it I shared the story of how I discovered that not only are the words of this blessing a beautiful expression of G-D's love toward us, but this prayer is the only one in the entire Bible written by the one true G-D of Israel. I encourage you to read *The Priestly Prayer of the Blessing* if you want the full story of this revelation and how I came to be chosen to impart this truth.

To increase your ability to receive the fullness of this impartation, this new book, *Praying the Priestly Prayer*, takes the insights I shared in my first book and delivers them in a month of shorter readings, helping you incorporate this prayer and its blessings into your daily life. My prayer is that it deepens your understanding of the prayer and helps you fully experience all its benefits. It's important to realize that it is possible to receive various degrees of benefit from anything written in the Bible. I've identified seven levels of blessing and understanding that are available to us:

1. One level of benefit comes from just reading the Word of G-D.
2. A second level is achieved by meditating on the Word.

3. An even greater blessing comes when we begin studying the connection of verses to other passages in the Bible.
4. An even deeper level occurs when we study the Hebrew or Greek meaning of the words themselves.
5. The fifth level is transformation, as the Word of G-D affects our very thinking.
6. A sixth and even deeper impact comes from G-D Himself as His Holy Spirit writes the meaning on our hearts.
7. But the seventh and greatest impartation comes when G-D manifests Himself—His very person—to us, dwells within us and upon us, and flows out from us to others. The result is a tangible change in our minds, hearts, souls, and circumstances, leading to supernatural breakthroughs!

Most believers either are not aware that deeper levels exist or have never been challenged to pursue such. They are unaware of the great blessings that ensue. When we receive the fullness of impartation, which G-D Himself intended to be experienced, there is no limit to what is possible! I believe you purchased this book because you want to go deeper in your understanding of this prayer and receive the fullness of everything G-D intends to impart through it, so let's get started.

The good news is that there are keys to how this divine prayer can be proclaimed effectively over us today, and the first key is realizing this Priestly Prayer of the Blessing is the only prayer written by the G-D of Israel Himself. The depth of this truth cannot be overstated. To grasp this, let's recall the circumstances into which G-D introduced this prayer.

G-D's Prayer of Grace in the Desert

The children of Israel had little understanding concerning the G-D who led them out of Egypt. As they crossed the Red Sea, they had little cognizance that they—the Hebrews enslaved by Egypt who were now free—were Abraham's physical descendants. The Old Testament had not yet been written—Moses was about to receive the first five books, the Torah, from the one true G-D of Israel on Mount Sinai.

They beheld ten plagues unleashed on Pharaoh and Egypt for not letting them go. They witnessed G-D parting the Red Sea and holding back the Egyptian army with a pillar of fire from heaven. They walked on dry ground as G-D made a pathway between two walls of raging water. And when they got to the other side, they watched as G-D caused the water to come crashing down with a vengeance on the Egyptian army pursuing them.

Yet while Moses was meeting with G-D on Mount Sinai, receiving His Word—His instructions, the Torah—they had Aaron build a golden calf and began worshipping this Egyptian idol. Moses was meeting with G-D on the top of Mount Sinai, receiving the Ten Commandments written by G-D's own finger, carved in stone.

G-D was angry with the children of Israel for worshipping the golden calf in the valley below. He told Moses that He would "wipe them out," but Moses interceded, and G-D repented of His anger against them.

It was to this rebellious, imperfect people, the children of Israel, that the one true G-D gave the supernatural Priestly Prayer of the Blessing for them to experience His reality in a personal and powerful way. G-D would soon tell Moses to have this prayer pronounced every day over the children of Israel by the high priest Aaron and Aaron's descendants.

Please don't miss the significance of what I'm saying. This wasn't a man's prayer to G-D; this was a prayer conceived by the G-D of Israel Himself to be prayed over His children. It is the greatest prayer of grace ever given to humanity. It is a supernatural prayer!

This prayer of blessing isn't based on how good or how perfect you are. The children of Israel weren't deserving of this, and neither are we. But this supernatural prayer was so powerful that it caused Israel to experience supernatural favor and blessing from G-D for forty years as they wandered in the wilderness. When proclaimed over you, this prayer will help propel you to be successful in all your endeavors.

PRAYER OF DECLARATION

G-D of Israel, I want to know You more deeply than I've ever known You before. Give me the ability to understand this prayer that You wrote. I thank You for showing me that You accept me as I am right now. I want to understand the truth and receive an impartation of Your presence like never before. I pray this in the name of Yeshua (Jesus).

Day 2

THE SIGNIFICANCE OF
THE HIGH PRIEST

They will put My name upon the children of Israel,
and I will bless them.

—Numbers 6:27

THE NEXT KEY to unlocking this prayer's effectiveness is to ask our-selves who G-D intended to proclaim this prayer of blessing every day over the children of Israel. Numbers 6:27, the verse immediately following the Priestly Prayer of the Blessing, answers this question and shows us why Israel received the outpouring of the supernatural that G-D intended.

Only the high priest could administer the Priestly Prayer of the Blessing because only he could dispense a supernatural impartation of the Shekinah glory onto the children of Israel—a portion that he received in the holy of holies. The high priest was an intermediary between the children of Israel and the one true G-D of Israel.

Why was an intermediary needed? An intercessor was always needed in the old covenant. At first, Moses would meet with the one true G-D on behalf of the children of Israel. Then, once the tabernacle in the wilderness was constructed as commanded by G-D Himself, and then the holy temple, only the high priest could meet directly with G-D in the holy of holies once a year as a representative of the people.

If the high priest was needed to impart this blessing under the old covenant, how can those of us under the new covenant receive the full impartation of the blessing today? I believe G-D has revealed to me how you and I can receive the same supernatural fullness that the children of Israel received through their high priest!

FROM OLD COVENANT TO NEW COVENANT

While pronouncing this blessing, the high priest Aaron extended his hands toward the people, spreading his fingers apart and placing his thumbs together to represent the Hebrew letter *shin*, an emblem for El Shaddai. This represented G-D Almighty. (The Hebrew word *dai* means to shed forth, pour out, or heap benefits.) By praying in this manner, through the high priest of Israel, a little portion of the actual Shekinah glory (the manifest presence of the one true G-D of Israel) was poured out on the children of Israel in a supernatural way.

There are two things to understand about the old covenant. First, the children of Israel did not have the Ruach HaKodesh (Holy Spirit) residing *within* them. The manifestation of the Holy Spirit within only occurred as a result of Yeshua's promise that it would be far better when He was gone because they would receive the indwelt Holy Spirit. (See John 14:16–17.)

The first promise resulting from the new covenant is that all believers who accept by faith Yeshua (Jesus) as their Messiah will have the Holy Spirit within them.

> Then I will sprinkle clean water upon you, and you shall be clean. From all your filthiness and from all your idols, I will cleanse you. Also, I will give you a new heart, and a new spirit [a new nature] I will put within you. And I will take away the stony heart out of your flesh, and I will give you a heart of flesh. *I will put My Spirit [Holy Spirit] within you* and cause you to walk in My statutes, and you will keep My judgments and do them.
>
> —EZEKIEL 36:25–27

Second, for the most part, the children of Israel didn't have the Holy Spirit *upon* them. Under the old covenant, the Holy Spirit was only placed upon certain individuals of Israel, such as prophets, kings, and priests. On one occasion, the Holy Spirit came upon a donkey ridden by the prophet Balaam, causing the donkey to speak and forbid the madness of the prophet (Num. 22:28).

The second promise from the new covenant was that all believers—not just appointed people such as prophets, kings, and priests—would one day have the Holy Spirit placed upon them, so they too could be witnesses and demonstrate G-D's kingdom on earth.

> And it shall come to pass afterward, that I will pour out my spirit upon all flesh; and your sons and your daughters shall prophesy, your old men shall dream dreams, your young men shall see visions: And also upon the servants and upon the handmaids in those days will I pour out my spirit.
>
> —JOEL 2:28–29, KJV

G-D gave Moses the Torah (G-D's written precepts, commandments, and instruction) to guide Israel in the covenant He had forged with them. The rabbis have deduced to the best of their corporate ability 613 different commandments. These were to be followed in "blind obedience"—no questions asked! If a person sinned against G-D, His grace was available for forgiveness through the sacrificial system of atonement and trespass offerings, which included the shedding of the blood of kosher (clean, unblemished) animals.

Truthfully, none of us could ever live up to such a high calling, especially without the Holy Spirit within us, except for the provision of grace, which in the old covenant was given through shedding the blood of unblemished animals. The old covenant's foundational truth that a sacrifice was needed to atone for our sins is also the new covenant's main foundational truth.

> For the life of the flesh is in the blood, and I have given it to you on the altar to make atonement for your lives; for it is the blood that makes atonement for the soul.
>
> —LEVITICUS 17:11

My point is that G-D did give the children of Israel something special, and He did not leave them without supernatural help. Through
this Priestly Prayer of the Blessing pronounced by the high priest over
them every day, G-D would be placing His very person (in the form
of a portion of the Shekinah glory) upon them in a supernatural way.
I contend that this was a different manifestation than what occurs
when one receives Yeshua as Messiah and Lord and when the Ruach
HaKodesh (Holy Spirit) comes to reside within (Ezek. 11:19; 36:26–
27) and the manifestation that occurs when the Holy Spirit comes
upon us (Joel 2:28–29).

This divine prayer imparts the same blessings today that it imparted
to the Israelites while they were in the wilderness: supernatural provision, supernatural health, angelic protection, and prosperity! Even
their shoes and clothes never wore out.

These miracles happened due to the high priest's proclamation of
the Priestly Prayer over them every day. Through the pronouncement
of this divine prayer in the manner prescribed by G-D Himself, a portion of the Shekinah glory was placed upon them.

Do you agree that it is still possible for us to receive this blessing? I
believe as you progress through the thirty days of this book, you will
discover that G-D wants us to experience the power of this priestly
prayer today.

PRAYER OF DECLARATION

*G-D of Israel, I come before You and ask that You continue to
let the revelation of this truth affect not only my intellect—my
mind—but I pray You write it on my heart so I will receive all
You have intended for me to experience! I pray this in the name
of Yeshua (Jesus).*

THE ONLY MEDIATOR

*There is one [G-D] and one mediator between [G-D] and men, the Man
[the Messiah Yeshua] Christ Jesus.*

—1 TIMOTHY 2:5

YESTERDAY WE EXPLORED the key of who G-D intended to pronounce this prayer of the blessing over the children of Israel. Since the fullness of the supernatural outpouring from this prayer comes only when pronounced by the Jewish high priest, there is a problem. How can we receive the full impartation of this blessing today—now—without a Jewish high priest proclaiming it over us every day? The good news is, though there isn't a Jewish high priest here on the earth today, there is a Jewish High Priest in heaven who desires to proclaim this prayer over us every day. His name is Yeshua (Jesus).

Yeshua as a Jewish High Priest doesn't have to perform all the things the high priest and the other priests (after the order of the Aaronic priesthood) had to do every morning according to Exodus 29. Yeshua doesn't have to make an offering for His sins, wash Himself with holy water from the bronze laver, or apply blood and oil on Himself. He is already holy and set apart to be the only intermediary between us and G-D the Father.

Aaron the high priest only had limited access into the holy of holies one day each year, during the feast of Yom Kippur (Day of Atonement). How much more will we receive an impartation of the person of G-D the Father when Yeshua—our High Priest who dwells in the true "holy of holies," seated at the right hand of the Father twenty-four hours a day, seven days a week—pronounces this prayer over us every day!

As the high priest in Moses' day, Aaron was the only mediator between G-D and humanity in the holy of holies on earth. So too

Yeshua (as our High Priest after Melchizedek's order) is the only mediator between G-D the Father and humanity in the heavenly holy of holies.

There is a holy temple in heaven with Yeshua, the Jewish High Priest, who is of a higher authority than the high priest after the order of the Aaronic priesthood. Yeshua wants to pray this prayer over you today and every day!

King David prophesied of this heavenly High Priest:

> The LORD said to my lord, "Sit at My right hand."...The LORD has sworn and will not change, "You are a priest forever after the order of Melchizedek."
>
> —PSALM 110:1, 4

Yeshua HaMashiach (Jesus the Messiah) is seated at the right hand of the one true G-D of Israel (the heavenly Father) in the heavenly holy of holies. His throne is the mercy seat in heaven. Yeshua's blood that He shed on the cursed tree was applied to this heavenly mercy seat so that we might receive forgiveness and become the children of G-D. (See Hebrews 4:14–16.)

At the last supper before His death and resurrection, Yeshua said the blessing over the bread and wine. This was the Hebrew blessing for the bread and the separate Hebrew blessing for the wine that all Jewish people are familiar with.

When Yeshua blessed the third cup of the Passover meal, which is known as the cup of blessing (or the cup of redemption), He said this cup should be remembered as representing His blood—the blood that would be shed for the institution of a new covenant, as promised in Jeremiah 31:31–33.

Yeshua's mission before the cross was to perfectly fulfill (observe) every one of G-D's commandments in the Torah without sinning once. He was the greatest old covenant prophet with the ability to heal, deliver, raise the dead, and perform miracles, signs, and wonders.

His main mission was to be the suffering Messiah who would die for us as the perfect sacrifice, the unblemished Lamb of G-D, who was prophesied about in the Tanakh (Old Testament) scriptures to die and rise again! With His resurrection, He became the firstfruits of many who would believe in Him as their Messiah. (See 1 Corinthians 15:20–23.)

The mission of Yeshua would change after His resurrection from the dead. It was the beginning of His priesthood. As the resurrected One, He walked with His disciples forty days after Passover. Standing on the Mount of Olives with His disciples before He ascended into heaven, Yeshua lifted both of His hands—the first time the Bible records Him lifting both hands—over them. Then it says that Yeshua proceeded to proclaim a blessing over them.

> Then He led them out as far as Bethany, and He lifted up His hands and blessed them. While He blessed them, He parted from them and was carried up into heaven. Then they worshipped Him, and returned to Jerusalem with great joy, and were continually in the temple, praising and blessing [G-D]. Amen.
>
> —Luke 24:50–53

What was this blessing that Yeshua said over them? Yeshua had spoken the Hebrew blessings over the bread and wine during the Passover meal—His last supper. Here He was standing before His disciples, lifting both hands. Only one prayer in Judaism requires raising both hands to proclaim a blessing. The high priest did this when he pronounced the Priestly Prayer of the Blessing over Israel. The high priest of Israel would lift his hands in the form of the El Shaddai (meaning G-D Almighty).

When I saw this truth, I was overcome with emotion, as I understood what Yeshua was doing as His last act of ministry on planet Earth. Yeshua lifted both His hands in Aaron the high priest's manner and pronounced the Priestly Prayer of the Blessing over the disciples. He didn't do this as a high priest after Aaron's order but as the resurrected One, performing this as the High Priest after the order of Melchizedek—an everlasting priesthood.

There is no better explanation of the blessing that Yeshua pronounced over them that day on the Mount of Olives. This was the first priestly function of Yeshua. And while He proclaimed it over them, He ascended before their eyes into the clouds to take His position—seated at the right hand of G-D the Father. Yeshua's throne is the heavenly mercy seat (the throne of mercy) in the heavenly holy of holies.

Yeshua desires to proclaim the Priestly Prayer of the Blessing over you so you too can receive the fullness of impartation available.

PRAYER OF DECLARATION

G-D of Israel, I realize that Yeshua (Jesus) is the One who will be praying the Priestly Prayer of the Blessing over me from His throne in the heavenly holy of holies. Through this divine prayer, I am ready to experience You, my heavenly Father, in a more intimate, experiential, and supernatural way. I thank You for helping me grasp the fullness of what You have in store for me today and in my future. I pray this in the name of Yeshua (Jesus).

THE POWER OF THE HEBREW LANGUAGE

I will put My law [Torah] within them and write it in their hearts.

—JEREMIAH 31:33

W E'VE LEARNED THE importance of why only the Jewish high priest was allowed to proclaim the divine prayer daily over the Israelites instead of Moses. I shared that though there is no Jewish high priest available on the earth today to pronounce this prayer over us, there is a Jewish High Priest available in heaven. Yeshua (Jesus) is our High Priest.

Now we are ready to explore the next important key to unlocking this prayer's full impartation: the Hebrew language. Several years ago G-D led me to create an amplified Hebrew-to-English translation of the prayer, which I shared in my book *The Priestly Prayer of the Blessing.* When I began to pronounce the prayer over myself every day, I was personally impacted in a manner like never before. I am convinced it is because of the fullness of meaning hidden in the Hebrew words. We are not receiving the fullness of impartation because the English translation we have in our Bibles lacks the full meaning, power, and anointing.

ABSTRACT AND CONCRETE WORDS

The English and Greek languages include many abstract words. In English the following words in italics are abstract:

> The LORD *bless* you and *keep* you; the LORD make His *face* to *shine* upon you, and be *gracious* unto you; the LORD *lift* His *countenance* upon you, and give you *peace*.
>
> —Numbers 6:24–26

What does it mean for G-D to bless us or to keep us? How does He make His face to shine on us? What does it mean that He will be gracious to us? How can He lift His countenance upon us? What does it mean by peace? These are abstract words, and we need to understand the Hebrew meaning to grasp fully what this prayer expresses.

Hebrew words have a depth of meaning that does not translate into the abstract language of English or other languages. Hebrew thought is concrete, meaning Hebrew words are related to the five senses: sight, smell, sound, taste, and touch. Hebrew isn't void of abstracts; however, the abstracts are related to something concrete. An abstract is something that cannot be experienced through the five senses.

> The judgments of the LORD are…sweeter also than honey and the honeycomb.
>
> —Psalm 19:9–10

> Oh, taste and see that the LORD is good.
>
> —Psalm 34:8

These verses refer to the Word of G-D being like honey to our souls. With the knowledge from his Jewish roots, Paul talks about praying from the deepest part of our being!

> Likewise, the Spirit helps us in our weaknesses, for we do not know what to pray for as we ought, but the Spirit Himself intercedes for us with groanings too deep for words.
>
> —Romans 8:26

When the enemy of our soul attacks us, we often sense emotional upheaval that manifests as a physical attack deep down in our bellies. Paul refers to the "bowels of mercies" in Colossians 3:12 as the place of deep-seated emotion. G-D can be experienced in the deepest level of our beings.

> Put on therefore, as the elect of [G-D], holy and beloved, bowels of mercies, kindness, humbleness of mind, meekness, long-suffering; forbearing one another, and forgiving one another, if any man have a quarrel against any: even as [the Messiah] forgave you, so also do ye.
> —Colossians 3:12–13, kjv

Mature believers use more than their minds!

> For everyone who partakes only of milk is unskilled in the word of righteousness, for he is a babe. But solid food belongs to those who are of full age, that is, those who by reason of use have their senses exercised to discern both good and evil.
> —Hebrews 5:13–14, nkjv

As a mature believer, you don't just have your mind trained to discern good and evil, but your senses have been exercised to discern the things of G-D. In other words, G-D can become so real to you that you can sense things as you drive in your car, enter a building, or hear someone talking. You may not have your Bible in front of you, but you can discern good and evil.

Some people say you should not go by feelings at all but only by what the Word of G-D says. Yet the Holy Spirit can communicate to us through our emotions, which are beyond the intellect and tangibly experienced by us. We can sense when someone is sharing with us something that isn't right. We can feel the presence of G-D when we worship. We can experience the joy or sadness that the Lord is allowing us to feel!

The Hebrew language deals with the meaning of words and

biblical concepts in the concrete, not just theoretical thinking. One of the main reasons Yeshua taught biblical concepts using parables was that the stories would give meaning to the truths more practically.

Tomorrow we will explore the first word we must understand in the Priestly Prayer of the Blessing—the actual sacred Hebrew name of the one true G-D of Israel. He has a name unlike any other name. There is power in His name. Those who are followers of the promised Jewish Messiah, Yeshua, understand there is power in His name too. Yet Yeshua Himself talked a lot of the power in the name of His Father, the one true G-D of Israel.

Prayer of Declaration

G-D of Israel, I ask that You allow me to encounter You more deeply as I learn the concrete concepts of this prayer that are rooted in the original Hebrew language. Please make Yourself real to me. I understand that one moment of Your presence can transform me, and I ask You to hear my prayer. I pray this in the name of Yeshua (Jesus).

SECTION II

~~~

MAY YHWH
BLESS YOU

~~~

DAY 5

THE SACREDNESS OF THE NAME

My name will be great among the nations.

—MALACHI 1:11

IN OUR ENGLISH Bibles, the word used for the name of G-D is LORD. It appears three times in the prayer of blessing. To more fully comprehend the power of the blessing and receive the full impartation of the divine prayer, we must first understand the very name being placed on us through its proclamation.

WHAT'S IN A NAME?

In most languages a name is a label, an identifier. My English name is Warren. It may have a deeper meaning, but we don't think of it as anything more than an identifier.

This is not the case in Hebrew. Behind every Hebrew name is a deeper meaning than the name itself. In Hebrew, each name is made up of words. For example, the name Ishmael is made of two Hebrew words: *shama*, meaning to hear, and *El*, meaning G-D. Thus, the name Ishmael means G-D hears.

The biblical pattern of naming children generally falls into one of three categories:

+ A child's name is given by G-D.
+ A child's name reflects the parent's prayer for the child.
+ A child's name reflects the circumstances or character of the child.

Thus, a person spends his whole life under the identity of his name. In this sense the names given to people in the Bible often prophesied who they would become.

G-D's real name as He identified Himself to Moses can be found in the Old Testament more than sixty-five hundred times. More than a label or identifier, it reveals something about His very nature and character. Therefore, we need to understand the meaning behind His name.

THE TETRAGRAMMATON

Understanding the meaning of G-D's name begins with an understanding of the tetragrammaton, the four Hebrew letters *Yod, Hey, Vov, Hey,* transliterated as YHWH.

Around the third century BC, Jewish rabbis began the tradition of not pronouncing G-D's sacred and holy name out of reverence for His holiness, which led to the tetragrammaton replacing the sacred name. By using only consonants and not revealing the vowels, its pronunciation has remained a mystery for many generations.

LORD Versus Lord

> The Jewish Masoretic text uses Adonai in the place of the tetragrammaton, YHWH. But in our English Bibles the tetragrammaton, YHWH, is translated as LORD. Notice that the use of small capital letters indicates it— LORD—as opposed to other names for G-D, which are translated using lowercase letters—Lord—elsewhere in the English Bible.

The sacred name is so holy as expressed in the tetragrammaton itself that to this day Orthodox Jews will substitute the Hebrew word Adonai (which means Lord) when they read it in the Holy Scriptures. Adonai is a beautiful expression of the one true G-D, but it isn't His sacred name as revealed to Moses. Yet even Adonai is too close to the sacred and holy name, according to some Orthodox Jews who won't say it in public. Instead, they will say in their conversations, "May

Hashem bless you." They will refer to Him in public as Hashem, which means *the name*. (Hashem comprises two words: *ha*, meaning the, and *shem*, meaning name.)

This causes a dilemma because many times in the Holy Scriptures the one true G-D of Israel declares that His sacred name shall be known. As I mentioned, the Old Testament refers to the sacred name of the one true G-D as represented in the tetragrammaton more than sixty-five hundred times. Therefore, I would submit to you that it is important to know what He revealed as His actual name. For only then can we communicate who the one true G-D is.

Since the tetragrammaton contains the consonants only of the sacred name (YHWH), to be able to pronounce the name of our heavenly Father, we need to know the vowels. For centuries the exact pronunciation has been a mystery. But theologians have agreed upon two possible conclusions arrived at by investigating several manuscript documents.

1. YeHoVaH (translated as Jehovah in some portions of the King James Version of the Bible)
2. YaHWeH

Many of us have read in the scriptures or shouted out in praise, "Hallelujah!" This Hebrew word is made up of two parts. *Hallelu* means praise. The second portion is actually an abbreviation of the sacred name of the heavenly Father. So when we say, "HalleluYAH," we are actually praising the sacred name of the one true G-D of Israel.

As a Jewish man who believes in Yeshua as my Messiah and Lord (Adonai), my relationship with G-D has changed. I am no longer simply a child of Israel—a child of the patriarchs Abraham, Isaac, and Jacob—but I am a spiritual son of G-D (YHWH, YeHoVaH, YaHWeH), my heavenly Father. We who believe in Yeshua have received access into the heavenly holy of holies to stand before the one true G-D, our heavenly Father. We can stand in the presence of the Almighty!

> Let us then come with confidence to the throne of grace, that we
> may obtain mercy and find grace to help in time of need.
> —Hebrews 4:16

Through the new birth, we have been adopted as spiritual sons and daughters of G-D. Because of Yeshua's sacrifice, we can come boldly before the throne of grace without fear of the name. In light of what Yeshua (Jesus) did for us, we don't have to be afraid to call on His name and pronounce the sacred name.

Although we have freedom under the new covenant, it is still important to understand the full meaning of what the Hebrew word *shem* implies to us. As with the rest of the Hebrew words in the prayer of blessing that I will be explaining, the Hebrew word *shem* means so much more than the word *name* means in English. For instance, one shade of the meaning is the Hebrew word *ne-shema*, which means breath.

This is part of the full understanding of the significance of having the name of G-D placed on us.

> Then the Lord [G-D] formed man from the dust of the ground and
> breathed into his nostrils the *breath of life*, and man [Adam] became
> a living being.
> —Genesis 2:7

When we read "the Lord [G-D]" in our English Bibles, the actual Hebrew word used isn't Lord but the tetragrammaton, YHWH, the sacred name of G-D. The Father breathed into Adam's nostrils; He was imparting a portion of His very person to Adam.

> Then [G-D] said, "Let us make man in our image, after our likeness,
> and let them have dominion over the fish of the sea, and over the

birds of the air, and over the livestock, and over all the earth, and over every creeping thing that creeps on the earth."

—Genesis 1:26

G-D the Father imparted the essence of who He is to His created son, Adam. How does this change your understanding of the G-D of Israel placing His name upon you?

Prayer of Declaration

Heavenly Father, I come before You in the name of Yeshua (Jesus). I thank You for revealing to me Your sacred name, YeHoVaH or YaHWeH. I praise You for sending Your only begotten Son, Yeshua, who made the way possible for me to become Your spiritual son or daughter.

Heavenly Father, I confess my love for You. Teach me how I can more fully love You in a more excellent way. Enable me through Your Holy Spirit to be able to love You with all my mind, my heart, my soul, my spirit, and my strength (substance). I pray that You remind me that You are present with me every moment of the day.

THE CHARACTER OF G-D

You shall not take the name of the LORD your [G-D]
in vain, for the LORD will not hold guiltless anyone
who takes His name in vain.

—EXODUS 20:7

TODAY WE WILL continue to explore G-D's name, focusing on how the Hebrew word *shem* for the English word *name* means character. In Hebraic thought, your *shem* (name) is your breath, and *your breath is your character.* It is your personality. It is what truly makes up who you are.

Let's look at how this changes a well-known concept, such as the second commandment, which teaches us not to take the name of the Lord in vain. If we replace the word *name* with the actual meaning in the scripture found in Exodus, it reads like this:

> You shall not take the [character] of the LORD your [G-D] in vain, for the LORD will not hold guiltless anyone who takes His [character] in vain.
>
> —EXODUS 20:7

Taking G-D's name in vain is not about adding a swear word to G-D's name. It's so much deeper. It's recognizing that, through Yeshua, G-D's name is upon us, and we must behave in a manner consistent with His character. We are to be examples of who the G-D of Israel truly is.

You see, in English we look at the word *name* in the abstract. When we read, "You shall not take the name of the LORD your G-D in vain," we surmise that it is talking about not using some curse word or profanity in conjunction with His name. Though it would be a good idea not to use His name as a curse word, the Hebrew meaning in this commandment refers to G-D's nature, His character, and the person who He truly is. It conveys that if we are G-D's children, we should not misrepresent who He is. We don't want to do those things that defile or discredit our heavenly Father and His holy character.

This is seldom being taught in the church today. Most don't realize what this scripture and others like it are truly conveying: you shall not falsely misrepresent the only one true G-D of Israel and the Messiah Yeshua (Jesus). In other words, taking G-D's name in vain is misrepresenting His character. If we confess Messiah, but we lie, cheat, and steal, then we are taking G-D's name (His *shem*, His character) in vain.

THE CHARACTER OF THE ONE TRUE G-D

Many people in the church today are on opposite sides concerning grace and holiness. The Scriptures declare:

> But as He who has called you is holy, so be holy in all your conduct, because it is written, "Be holy, for I am holy."
>
> —1 PETER 1:15–16

G-D the Father, Yeshua, and the Ruach HaKodesh (Holy Spirit) are persons of the Elohim (the triune nature of G-D). Just as we have things we love and things we dislike or even hate, so too does G-D. In the Torah, G-D calls the things He loves holy and the things He hates sin. If we do the things He loves and calls holy, we will have victory, provision, good health, prosperity, unity, peace, safety, perfect love, everlasting life, and much more. Things He calls sin will bring strife, sickness, failure, poverty, war, loneliness, despair, suicide, everlasting condemnation, and much more.

If we want to have a good and intimate relationship with

another person, the first thing we do is learn the things they love and the things they hate. We then intentionally try to do those things that bring us closer, and we avoid those things that would divide us.

The moral precepts of the Law (the Torah) are still intact. Things G-D lists as being holy were not changed when the new covenant was ushered in because they reflect His character, and the character of the one true G-D never changes. The Bible says:

> For I am the LORD, I do not change.
>
> —MALACHI 3:6

> Jesus Christ [Yeshua the Messiah] is the same yesterday, and today, and forever.
>
> —HEBREWS 13:8

G-D's character—His attributes or perfections—doesn't change. He is always good, loving, just, righteous, holy, all-knowing, and all-powerful. Let me assure you that knowing the name and the character of the one true G-D as your heavenly Father will help you enter a deeper, life-changing relationship with Him. After all, your heavenly Father is the One who authored this unparalleled supernatural prayer! To know your heavenly Father by His name will cause you to have faith to believe Him for the impossible!

Remember, the Hebrew word for *name* is *shem*. When G-D places His *shem* upon us, He is actually imparting His very breath, His holy character, His power and authority upon us! Just as Father G-D breathed into the nostrils of Adam, who was formed out of the clay of the earth, so too when the Priestly Prayer of the Blessing is pronounced over us, we receive an impartation of the heavenly Father.

PRAYER OF DECLARATION

Heavenly Father, I thank You not only for revealing to me Your sacred name but also that You desire for me to receive an impartation of Your name (Your shem) upon me through Your divine prayer of the blessing.

May You impart to me Your very breath, Your holy character, Your power and authority. I ask You for this in the name of Your only begotten Son, Yeshua (Jesus).

THE NAME OF G-D

In every place incense will be offered to My name, and a pure offering. For
My name will be great among the nations, says the LORD of hosts.

—MALACHI 1:11

TODAY WE WILL cover an important key to the prayer of blessing:
not just knowing *about* your heavenly Father but instead getting
to truly *know* Him and have access to Him in a supernatural, experiential, and intimate way.

How can we truly say we have intimacy with someone if we don't
know that person's name? How can we declare we *know* G-D if we
don't comprehend how much He loves us and how calling on His
name will forever change every moment of every day of the rest of
our lives?

Today we'll look at what makes the name of G-D different from all
other gods. Our English word *god* is very broad; it can mean any deity,
including false gods. However, the one true G-D of Israel identifies
Himself with an actual name.

Many believers do not understand the one true G-D and His
actual name well enough to explain them to others. If we can understand who we are praying to and how glorious He truly is—His character and what He can do because of His attributes—we won't be
afraid, struggling with so many issues. We will increase our faith and
peace knowing that we have a "big Daddy." Through Him nothing is
impossible!

It's important to know His name—because there is only one true
G-D. This is made known in the Ten Commandments, which say:

You shall have no other gods before Me. You shall not make for
yourself any graven idol, or any likeness of anything that is in heaven
above, or that is in the earth beneath, or that is in the water below
the earth. You shall not bow down to them or serve them; for I, the
LORD your [G-D], am a jealous [G-D], visiting the iniquity of the
fathers on the children to the third and fourth generation of them
who hate Me.

—EXODUS 20:3–5

When we understand who our heavenly Father truly is, we begin
to grasp the power and glory we can be part of while living on earth.
If we are in Yeshua—we believe in Him and have been born again—
then by default when we pray to the Father, we are praying to the
one true G-D of Israel. When we pray to the Father in the name of
Yeshua, even without understanding who our heavenly Father truly
is—holy, above all things, all-powerful—by default we are praying to
the one true G-D of Israel.

For you have not received the spirit of slavery again to fear. But you
have received the Spirit of adoption, by whom we cry, "Abba, Father."

—ROMANS 8:15

Abba is the Hebrew term for Daddy. It's OK to view yourself as a
little child when you go before your heavenly Father.

And because you are sons, [G-D] has sent forth into our hearts the
Spirit of His Son, crying, "Abba, Father!"

—GALATIANS 4:6

Sometimes we do not know how to pray, especially when we go
through the heaviest trials, feeling low and unable to even lift our
Bibles to read. But in those times, we can go before our heavenly
Father and allow the Ruach HaKodesh (Holy Spirit) to pray through
us with words we don't understand.

> Likewise, the Spirit helps us in our weaknesses, for we do not know
> what to pray for as we ought, but the Spirit Himself intercedes for
> us with groanings too deep for words.
>
> —ROMANS 8:26

When it comes to fully understanding the significance of the
Priestly Prayer of the Blessing, the Ruach HaKodesh (Holy Spirit)
helps us understand the Hebrew meaning of the words. Hence, we
fully appreciate and comprehend how powerful and profound the
prayer truly is.

We are commanded in Holy Scriptures to proclaim His true name,
the sacred name of the one true G-D of Israel, the name concealed in
the tetragrammaton, that of YeHoVaH, or YaHWeH.

> For from the rising of the sun to its setting, *My name* will be great
> among the nations, and in every place incense will be offered to *My
> name*, and a pure offering. For *My name* will be great among the
> nations, says the LORD of hosts.
>
> —MALACHI 1:11

This scripture is clear that all nations are to understand the name
of the one true G-D. Yeshua came to show forth exactly who the
one true G-D is. Yeshua was a manifestation of the character of the
Father for all to witness and comprehend!

> Thus says [YHWH], the Maker of the earth, [YHWH] who
> formed it to establish it; [YHWH] is His name: Call to Me, and I
> will answer you, and show you great and mighty things which you
> do not know.
>
> —JEREMIAH 33:2–3

So the hidden sacred name of the one true G-D is actually in the
original Hebrew Scriptures. In the Scriptures, G-D calls out to us,
imploring us to seek Him as our heavenly Father and petition Him
in prayer.

How do you call out to someone without knowing his or her name? If my wife and I are separated in a crowded room and she wants to communicate with me, it is helpful that she can call out my name: "Warren, where are you?"

What about when we need prayer? If I don't know another person's name, I might say, "Hey brother, can I ask you to pray with me about something?" It's far better if I know that person's name. Why? Because when I don't know another person's actual name, my relationship remains at a distance.

The same principle applies to our relationship with G-D. If we say we have an intimate relationship with the one true G-D yet we don't truly know His name, how intimate are we?

PRAYER OF DECLARATION

Heavenly Father, I call upon Your sacred name, YeHoVaH, or YaHWeH. I thank You for revealing to me that You are the one true G-D. There is no other like You! I confess how awesome and holy You truly are. I realize that in the Tanakh (Old Covenant), only the high priest (after the order of Aaron) could come into Your presence in the holy of holies once a year, the Day of Atonement (Yom Kippur). Yet through Your only begotten Son, Yeshua, my High Priest (after the everlasting order of Melchizedek) can I now come boldly into Your heavenly throne room and not only address You by Your sacred name but call You Abba, Father.

Help me by the power of Your Ruach HaKodesh (Holy Spirit) to remember that I am Your spiritual son or daughter. Remind me that I can call upon Your name anytime and receive Your help in times of trouble or prosperity. May You give me Your direction and impart Your assignments. I ask for these things in the name of Yeshua.

THE NAME OF YESHUA

I will do whatever you ask in My name.

—John 14:13

In English we call our Messiah and Lord "Jesus Christ." This is a label—an identifier—but it doesn't convey the attributes, character, or deeper meaning behind the name itself as contained in Hebrew. The word Christ isn't His name; it is His title.

The English translation of Jesus Christ came from the Greek, Yesous Cristos. Christ is the Greek word for *messiah* (HaMashiach in Hebrew) or the anointed one. Jesus' name in Hebrew is accepted as Yeshua. In His full name and title, Yeshua HaMashiach, we have a revelation of His attributes and character.

Yeshua (Yahu'Shuah) means YHWH saves. The sacred name of G-D is alluded to in Jesus' Hebrew name! You would never know that by His English name. Yeshua came to represent the Father. In the Hebrew name Yeshua the Messiah (the Christ) we have both His divinity as the only begotten Son of YHWH and the humanity of Him as Messiah (the anointed prophet). Yeshua is 100 percent G-D and 100 percent man. This reality is expressed within the Hebrew name but lost in the English translation.

The full name of Yeshua HaMashiach (Jesus the Christ) means the one true G-D saves as the anointed one—the prophet. He has provided us with direct access to the Father, and there is never any changing of this truth. Like YHWH (YeHoVaH or YaHWeH), Yeshua's being, nature, character, purposes, promises, and plans can be counted on, for He is faithful and true. He is the rock that we can build on, the One we can trust in this ever-changing world because He is one with the unchangeable G-D.

We've Been Given a New Name

In Yeshua we have been named with a new name. The name and character of our old man (nature) have been exchanged for the "breath of new life." As we walk with Yeshua, we have the covering of the name (HaShem) and the actual person of G-D on us and within us, by the power of the Ruach HaKodesh (Holy Spirit).

When we take Yeshua's name upon us, we are called to be imitators of the Messiah. This doesn't come by our striving to become more like Him, but it comes through being in a relationship with Him and having His character imparted to us by the power of the Ruach HaKodesh (Holy Spirit).

The time we spend in worship, prayer, and the Word (the Bible) causes us to obtain the power to become more like Yeshua. We cannot attain His likeness on our own but only through the power of the Ruach HaKodesh (Holy Spirit) within us.

The Power of Praying in Yeshua's Name

> I will do whatever you ask in My name, that the Father may be glorified in the Son.
>
> —John 14:13

Many interpret this as if there is *magic* in the name of Yeshua. There is *power* in the name of Yeshua. But praying in His name means something far more! If we properly interpreted the English word *name* from the Hebrew and Greek and substituted it for the word *name* in this verse, it would read:

> I will do whatever you ask in My *character*, that the Father may be glorified in the Son.

If you ask G-D for something that is not in His character, you can be sure He will not do it. If you do receive what you asked for, but it is against that which G-D calls holy, you didn't get it from G-D; you got it from the enemy.

How did Yeshua glorify the Father? By doing the things the Father would have done on earth, by remaining consistent with the Father's character.

The Greek word for *name* (*onoma*) used in John 14:13 is consistent with the Hebrew word *shem*. *Onoma* means "the manifestation or revelation of someone's character…distinguishing them from all others."[1] Thus, "praying in the name of Yeshua (Jesus)" means to pray as directed (authorized) by Him, bringing revelation that flows *out of His being when you are in His presence*!

Therefore, praying in Yeshua's name is not a religious formula just to end prayers or a magic word to get what we want! Praying in His name is praying in His actual person, with His holy character, power, and authority. If G-D answers your prayer, then He is the One who receives all the glory, not you!

In Acts 19:13–16 we read about a group of Jewish men who went about trying to drive out evil spirits from other Jewish brethren. They tried to invoke the name of Yeshua (Jesus) over a man who was demon possessed. They said, "In the name of Yeshua (Jesus), whom Paul preaches, I command you to come out."

The demon within the man spoke back to them, "Yeshua (Jesus) I know, and I know about Paul, but who are you?"

Then the evil spirit jumped out of the man and overpowered them. The demon beat them, and they ran out of the house naked and bleeding.

They had prayed in the name of Yeshua (Jesus), hadn't they? Why didn't they get the same results as Paul or the disciples when they used the same methodology to cast out demons? It's because they weren't born-again. They didn't have an intimate relationship with the living

Messiah. The demon recognized that these men had no authority or power over it.

Many believers aren't walking in the supernatural power of G-D because many don't feel worthy of being used by Him in this way. The truth is, none of us are worthy enough. But G-D wants to use you if you are willing to pray in His person, with His holy character, power, and authority, making sure He gets all the glory and honor!

Now that you understand the powerful meaning of the name of G-D and Yeshua, we are ready to break down the next word in the prayer of blessing and reveal its deeper meaning as conveyed in the original Hebrew.

Prayer of Declaration

I thank You, heavenly Father, for revealing Yourself in the person of Your only begotten Son, Yeshua (Jesus). Now I know that every time I pray in the name of Yeshua, I am praying as directed (authorized) by You, Father. I bring my request to You, being in unity with Yeshua seated at Your right hand. Father, Your power and authority are made known through the person of Yeshua and made alive in me through the power of the Ruach HaKodesh (Holy Spirit).

I now make these specific prayer requests to You, heavenly Father, in the name of Yeshua. (Ask for what you need from the Father.)

THE HEBREW WORD FOR *BLESS*

The LORD bless you.

—NUMBERS 6:24

T HE GOAL OF today's reading is that you will come to better understand the meaning of the English word *bless*, which is an abstract concept. Think about it. What does it mean to bless? Without this understanding, you cannot receive the full impartation of what this divine prayer can usher into your life.

In Hebrew the word for *bless* is *barakh*. We can better understand this abstract word's meaning by looking into how it is used in other Scripture passages.

> He made his camels kneel down [*barakh*] outside the city by a well
> of water in the evening when the women came out to draw water.
> —GENESIS 24:11

The camel kneels so the person can receive the gifts on its back. Figuratively, kneeling to help someone pick up something they have dropped is also blessing them.

This first portion of the Priestly Prayer of the Blessing communicates that the one true G-D of Israel (the heavenly Father) is kneeling in front of you with His arms outstretched, making Himself available to you in a way you never thought possible. You will experience the greatest intimacy possible with YHWH (your heavenly Father) and receive all the gifts He wants to impart to you.

This first portion of the Priestly Prayer of the Blessing involves G-D our Father making Himself available to each of us. As such, it demands a response. Do we ignore Him? Do we stand and stare at Him kneeling in front of us? No! We are moved to respond in our

hearts, humbling ourselves and falling to our knees so we can receive
His invitation! A child seeing his good father or mother kneeling in
front of him would know that what comes next is their loving embrace.

The one true G-D of Israel wants to come down from His heavenly throne to be with you. This occurs when the prayer of blessing is
pronounced over you in the name of the Jewish High Priest Yeshua
(Jesus).

The concrete or extended meaning of the Hebrew word *barakh*
is to do or give something of value to another. G-D blesses you by
making Himself available. He wants to provide for your needs, and
you in turn bless G-D by giving Him yourself in submission as He
kneels in front of you with His outstretched arms of love.

Many of us need healing, deliverance, salvation, financial relief,
or some other breakthrough! We often turn to G-D in our times of
trouble and ask Him to answer our prayers. We move from one need
to the next. But Yeshua talked about why we shouldn't be anxious
about our daily needs. (See Matthew 6:25–32.)

The key statement made in Matthew 6 is that YHWH, your heavenly Father, knows what you need before you even ask. What must
you do to receive such favor of the Father?

> But seek first the kingdom of [G-D] and His righteousness, and all
> these things shall be given to you.
>
> —MATTHEW 6:33

According to Yeshua, to gain favor from the Father, we must "seek
first the kingdom of [G-D]." Many books and teachings have been created about the kingdom of G-D. Still, I believe most convey a mis-
understanding of what Yeshua was referring to. When Yeshua said,
"Seek first the kingdom of [G-D] and His righteousness, and all these
things shall be given to you," He was conveying that we are to seek
the kingdom of G-D not as an end in itself but because the King is
there. He was referring to obtaining an intimate relationship with the

one true G-D of Israel. When we are in the presence of our heavenly Father, we receive everything we need by default. We don't even have to ask because He, as a good Father, is with us and already discerns what we are lacking.

So many of us live from one need to another. We seek G-D's hand of provision instead of seeking His face. In 2 Chronicles 7:14, YHWH gives us a formula for truly obtaining healing and even revival to invade our land:

> If My people, who are called by My name, will humble themselves and pray, and seek My face and turn from their wicked ways, then I will hear from heaven, and will forgive their sin and will heal their land.

Imagine what G-D is saying here! People first need to humble themselves. To humble oneself in the Hebrew sense is to come to the end of yourself and confess that you don't have all the answers, the power, or the means to survive without G-D in your life. The best way to describe it is receiving an epiphany or having an aha moment of revelation. King David humbled himself often before almighty G-D in his psalms.

> Be gracious to me, O LORD, for I am weak; O LORD, heal me, for my bones are terrified. My soul is greatly troubled, but You, O LORD, how long?
>
> —PSALM 6:2–3

> I am weary with my groaning; all night I flood my bed with weeping; I drench my couch with my tears. My eye wastes away from grief; it grows weak because of all those hostile to me.
>
> —PSALM 6:6–7

The injunction laid out by G-D in 2 Chronicles 7:14, after we humble ourselves, is to pray—to start communicating with our heavenly Father and talking with Him. But it doesn't end there. Most of us have come to the Lord at one time or another and prayed to Him. But the next part of that scripture is truly different. The Father tells His people to seek His face. This is a call to deep intimacy.

If the Father asks us to seek His face, doesn't this mean that we can have access to Him in the most intimate way? YHWH would not be so cruel as to tease us, saying, "Seek My face," but then continue to hide from us. G-D is not a liar!

Our heavenly Father is saying, "I want you to approach Me, to come into My presence. I want you to allow Me to be with you, to share My love with you. You have been distant, caught up in your busy life, yet here I am right in front of you—I want you to know how much I love you. I am waiting for you to tell Me, 'I love you, Daddy (Abba)!'"

Satan hates the heavenly Father. Why? Because Satan was thrown out of heaven by the Father for rebelling against Him! Satan's main objective is to keep us away from intimacy with the Father. Yeshua has already defeated the devil at the cross. By recognizing Yeshua as our Messiah and Lord (Adonai), we can gain intimacy with Him and sense His presence as we commune with Him. Satan cannot stop the Ruach HaKodesh (Holy Spirit) from doing the work He is performing in our lives once we have been born again. But if Satan could somehow discredit the heavenly Father and keep us from accessing Him, then he has a chance of thwarting our G-D-given destiny and purpose.

Many of us do not understand what Yeshua did on the cross for us. He broke down the middle partition, the veil, separating us from access to G-D the Father in the heavenly holy of holies. After many of us come to know Yeshua as Messiah and Lord (Adonai), we look on that as a one-time encounter. As years go by, we lose the understanding that the "born-again experience" wasn't meant to be a one-time event, but rather it was our entranceway into an ongoing intimacy with the one true G-D of Israel.

Even though some of us enter into a deeper relationship with G-D through the person of the Holy Spirit and communion with Yeshua, many times we partition our lives between our church fellowships, Bible studies, or worship services and our ongoing day-to-day lives. For the most part we put spiritual things aside to attend to our worldly affairs. We don't realize it, but we live from crisis to crisis— from one need to another—because our moment-by-moment journey is lived separated from the One who wants to provide the very best for us: YHWH (YeHoVaH, YaHWeH, our heavenly Father).

To *bless* in Hebrew means that the Father has left His heavenly abode and wants to kneel in front of you, making Himself available to you—not just for you to receive the good things that He desires to give you, but He kneels in front of you as an invitation for you to be with Him. He wants to place His name (*shem*) on you. YHWH wants to supernaturally place a portion of His very person, His holy character, and His power and authority on you. He is right in front of you, but it is up to you to respond to His presence by faith.

PRAYER OF DECLARATION

Heavenly Father, I accept Your invitation. I ask for forgiveness for not recognizing the fact that You desire fellowship with me. It was as if I were living in a spiritual orphanage. I knew You were my heavenly Father, but I lived apart from You, never confessing my love and appreciation of You. Thank You for making Yourself so accessible through Your Priestly Prayer of the Blessing. I want to get to know You in a greater way than ever before. I worship and praise Your holy name.

THE DEEPER MEANING OF *BARAKH*

[Yeshua], knowing that the Father had given all things into His hands and
that He came from [G-D] and was going to [G-D], rose from supper, laid
aside His garments, and took a towel and wrapped Himself. After that,
He poured water into a basin and began to wash the disciples' feet and to
wipe them with the towel with which He was wrapped.

—JOHN 13:3–5

TODAY WE WILL further explore the deeper meaning of the Hebrew word *barakh*. We see the meaning of *barakh* through what Yeshua did during His final Passover Seder with His disciples in John 13:3–5. Yeshua, who represents G-D the Father in the form of His only begotten Son, is on His knees washing the disciples' feet. Yeshua provides a perfect picture of *barakh* (to bless) by kneeling in front of another.

It appears that the disciples felt uncomfortable with this. They must have thought this was beneath the Messiah's dignity. He shouldn't be kneeling in front of them, washing their feet; instead, they should be doing this for Him.

Yeshua desired to teach Peter and the other disciples how to bless others by being a servant. The Messiah explained that if Peter wouldn't allow Yeshua to bless him by washing his feet, Peter could not have any true relationship with Yeshua. Peter suddenly changed his mind concerning Yeshua kneeling before him and responded, "Then don't just wash my feet, but give my whole body a bath!"

Yeshua was demonstrating the meaning of *barakh*. In the same way, YHWH's intention in the Priestly Prayer of the Blessing is, "I want to bless (*barakh*) you. I want to kneel in front of you, My son or My daughter, and make Myself available to you, and by your receiving Me, you will receive all I have for you!"

CONNECTING WITH YHWH LIKE NEVER BEFORE

Many believers have a personal relationship with Yeshua and the Holy Spirit. Many have by faith received Yeshua as their Messiah and Lord (Adonai). Through repentance and a simple prayer of salvation they have supernaturally begun to experience Yeshua's presence in their lives. Others have received a deeper, experiential, and supernatural relationship with the Ruach HaKodesh (Holy Spirit) through an encounter with Him. Some refer to this event as the "baptism of the Holy Spirit," while others call it an awakening, revival, or renewal.

Yet it has been difficult for many of us to relate to YHWH (our heavenly Father) intimately and experientially. Through religion, we often view YHWH (our heavenly Father) as seated on His throne in heaven, holy, unapproachable, and surrounded by twenty-four elders and a myriad of angels on their faces worshipping Him. Although those things are true, it is also true that He authored this divine prayer to help us connect with Him in a supernatural, intimate, and experiential way like never before.

Once we embrace Him and He embraces us, all the promises and gifts He wants to bestow on us are imparted to us. This is a result of having Him in our lives in a very real way. Not only can we have intimacy with Yeshua and the Ruach HaKodesh (Holy Spirit), but now we can also have full access in a supernatural way to YHWH (our heavenly Father).

This is the way to begin a relationship with what I call the fullness of the Elohim (Godhead, triune nature of G-D, Three in One)! Many are expecting a great move of G-D to invade planet Earth. They say it will not be like any other revival that occurred before! As a student of revivals, I couldn't imagine how this next great end-time revival could be different from any other! Most moves are similar to ones that have occurred before. But I believe the Lord has shown me that the difference in this next revival will be in YHWH (our heavenly Father) revealing Himself in a way like never before—in the manifestation of the fullness of the Shekinah glory. For those of us who enter in, we will be walking in a far greater outpouring of the supernatural power of G-D. Yeshua said we would do "greater works [or miracles]" than He did (John 14:12). This will happen as a result of our walking in the fullness of the Elohim (the Father, Son, and Holy Spirit).

Religion often places separation, or distance, between G-D and us. It portrays YHWH (our heavenly Father) as too holy to be approached. The truth is, the one true G-D of Israel, King of the universe, loves His spiritual sons and daughters and desires to come down from His throne in heaven, making Himself available to us in a tangible way. We often forget that He is omnipresent, meaning that He can be present everywhere at all times. Many times in the Holy Scriptures, YHWH (the heavenly Father) Himself left His heavenly throne and came to reveal Himself to an undeserving people!

We have only touched the surface of the full implications concerning this first portion of the Priestly Prayer of the Blessing. Because it is so important to grasp this truth, tomorrow we will further explore this ultimate doorway to G-D's blessing.

PRAYER OF DECLARATION

Heavenly Father, I thank You for making Yourself available to me. More than that, through the pronouncement of the first portion of this divine prayer, You are making Yourself available to me in a way I never could have imagined. It's hard for me to grasp that You want to kneel down in front of me with Your arms outstretched. I should be doing that before You.

Help me to awaken to the reality that You love me so much that not only do You reside in heaven on Your throne, but You are omnipresent and able to make Yourself available to me here on the earth.

I pray in the name of Yeshua (Jesus) that You assist me in recognizing Your presence in my everyday life. Help me to overcome by Your Ruach HaKodesh (Holy Spirit) any negative views of fatherhood based on the failures and imperfections of my earthly parents. I forgive my earthly father and mother for their inability to live up to their purpose and calling of parenting me. May they too discover the reality of knowing You as their heavenly Father in a new, powerful way.

Day 11

THE ULTIMATE DOORWAY

*I am the way, the truth, and the life. No one comes to
the Father except through Me.*

—John 14:6

WHAT DOES THE prayer of blessing mean when it says that
YHWH wants to bless us? Is it hard to accept that the one
true G-D of heaven and earth, YHWH (your heavenly Father), leaves
His heavenly throne in some cosmic fashion to kneel before us to offer
Himself to us?

This first portion of the Priestly Prayer of the Blessing is the most
significant part of the prayer—it is the ultimate doorway to receive
all the gifts and promises from heaven! G-D the Father is making
Himself available to you! Is it too hard to accept this unmerited favor?

Religion wants to keep our heavenly Father away from our access;
theologians believe we aren't worthy of being in His presence. Many
Christian theologians stress having an intimate relationship with
Yeshua and the Ruach HaKodesh (Holy Spirit) but still place encum-
brances between the Father and us.

Religion says it is better to approach G-D through intermediaries
such as priests, pastors, rabbis, or special emissaries called saints who
have died and are now in heaven. We are told we must bring offerings (not bulls and goats but financial offerings) and perform acts
of penance to gain G-D's favor. But no matter what we do, religion
never allows us to get closer because religion raises fences and encum-
brances that hinder us from direct access.

The tragedy is that Yeshua paid a brutal price on the cross that we
might have direct access to the heavenly Father.

For [Yeshua] is our peace, who has made both groups one and has broken down the barrier of the dividing wall.

—Ephesians 2:14

The "dividing wall" refers to ordinances under the old covenant that separated the Israelites from other nations and from YHWH, who dwelt in the holy of holies in the form of the Shekinah glory. The dividing wall is typified by the veil in the tabernacle and later the holy temple, which divided the holy place from the holy of holies.

When Yeshua was on the cross, He cried out, "It is finished" (John 19:30), and then He said, "Father, into Your hands I commit My spirit" (Luke 23:46). He breathed His last breath and died. The veil in the holy temple was rent from top to bottom. Theologians say it symbolizes breaking down the dividing wall of separation, granting every believer in Yeshua access to the heavenly holy of holies. (See Hebrews 10:19–20.)

Theologians state that Yeshua's body being torn by the nails as He hung on the cross caused the veil to be torn so that we who believe in Yeshua as our Messiah and Lord now have access by faith to YHWH (our heavenly Father) in the heavenly throne room.

But I also believe that the veil was torn to indicate that YHWH can now come out to meet with His spiritual sons and daughters. Sin separated the heavenly Father from humanity because we were all marked with the stain of original sin. But Yeshua dealt with sin on the cross through His death as the "Lamb of [G-D], who takes away the sin of the world" (John 1:29). The Bible says concerning those of us who are under the new covenant:

[YHWH] made [Yeshua] who knew no sin to be sin for us, that we might become the righteousness of [G-D] in Him.

—2 Corinthians 5:21

This means that now YHWH (our heavenly Father) can also come down to earth from His holy of holies in heaven and approach His spiritual sons and daughters through His Priestly Prayer of the Blessing. Why? Because we who accept Yeshua have been made holy through the blood sacrifice of Yeshua.

Are you beginning to comprehend how G-D truly has reached out to make a way for intimacy with humanity time and time again? The most remarkable thing YHWH did was come down from His heavenly throne to earth, making Himself known in a bodily form through Yeshua, His only begotten Son.

When one would look into Yeshua's face, one would be beholding the face of the heavenly Father in a palatable form. G-D told Moses, who desired intimacy with Him, that he could not see the face of YHWH, or he would surely die. But when a person looked at the face of Yeshua, they were peering into the face of the heavenly Father, and instead of dying, they received life everlasting!

The Hebrew word *barakh* implies the ultimate gift of the coming of YHWH (our heavenly Father) from His heavenly throne to the earth and making Himself available to us in the form of Yeshua, the Messiah Himself. Yeshua said, "I am the way, the truth, and the life. No one comes to the Father except through Me" (John 14:6).

Yeshua was the ultimate way in which YHWH (our heavenly Father) would make Himself available to us—until He comes to earth, along with Yeshua, in fulfillment of the prophecy in Revelation 21. Many talk about Yeshua's second coming, but Yeshua isn't the only one returning to earth when the New Jerusalem comes down from heaven. (See Revelation 21:22–27.)

Can you understand how this first portion of the Priestly Prayer of the Blessing can become a stumbling block to some? The people who struggle with this first part of the amplified Hebrew-to-English translation must understand that YHWH, though holy and unapproachable, has continually reached out to embrace us with a desire to save us, redeem us, deliver us, heal us, and adopt us as His spiritual sons and daughters.

> For [G-D the Father] so loved the world that He gave His only begotten Son, that whoever believes in Him should not perish, but have eternal life.
>
> —John 3:16

What does it mean that Yeshua was G-D's only begotten Son? Adam (the first man) was YHWH's created son. YHWH intended to create man in His likeness and image. How did He do this with Adam? It was G-D the Father who created Adam out of the clay of the earth. He then breathed into Adam's nostrils and imparted His DNA, His very breath, His holy character, and His power and authority.

The difference between Adam and Yeshua is that Adam was created and Yeshua was begotten. *Begotten* means YHWH sent His pure and holy seed into the womb of Miriam (Mary) and impregnated her. By Yeshua having the holy blood of the heavenly Father, He was born without the stain of Adam's original sin. Adam had no mother, but he had YHWH as his Father, who created him and then breathed His life into him. On the other hand, Yeshua (Jesus) was YHWH's physical Son, created by His seed planted in Miriam's womb. Which do you think was harder, the heavenly Father breathing His breath into Adam's nostrils or planting His holy seed into the womb of Miriam? Nothing is impossible for the one true G-D of Israel, the Creator of the universe!

When Yeshua took the beatings and the thirty-nine stripes from the Roman whip called the cat-o'-nine-tails, He did so to take your sickness upon Himself. But it wasn't only the Messiah who took this beating for you; it was YHWH (your heavenly Father) too!

The rabbinic extrabiblical writings talk about how YHWH can

sense the pain, sickness, and sorrows that we as His people are facing. It is surmised that if He allowed one tear to fall from His eye, the entire earth would be flooded. These writings convey in a powerful way that YHWH has empathy for us.[1]

This implies that it wasn't only Yeshua who took your shame, your guilt, and your sin upon Himself as He hung on the cross—but YHWH (your heavenly Father) was vicariously suffering on that cross through His only begotten Son. Yeshua's holy blood shed for us on the cross was the very same blood of YHWH. The Torah states:

> For the life of the flesh is in the blood, and I have given it to you on the altar to make atonement for your lives; for it is the blood that makes atonement for the soul.
>
> —LEVITICUS 17:11

It was the holy blood of YHWH (our heavenly Father) that flowed through Yeshua's veins. G-D's sole seed was placed into the womb of Yeshua's mother, Miriam (Mary), to conceive the only begotten Son. Yeshua paid the price of your sin so you can become born again—an adopted son or daughter of the Most High G-D.

It was YHWH Himself who came in the form of His only begotten Son and vicariously suffered. YHWH (our heavenly Father) also was reviled by men and beaten. The Father could identify with His only begotten Son, Yeshua, whose arms were outstretched—held by the nails of crucifixion! Yeshua died a horrible death on the cross. G-D the Father could sense every pain that His Son suffered for us in this brutal death sentence. In light of this, how can we ever question whether YHWH (our heavenly Father) would kneel before us with outstretched hands, beckoning us to come to Him so He can enfold us with His divine embrace?

There is no good reason to refuse to accept that through this first portion of the prayer of blessing, YHWH wants to come down from His heavenly throne to kneel before you, His son or daughter, to minister to you and to impart a portion of Himself to you! YHWH so loves you. He even came in the form of His only begotten Son to take the punishment you deserved and died in your place to take away your sin!

Do you see now why YHWH chose to write this portion as the first part of His divine prayer of the blessing: "The Lord (YHWH) bless you"? If you can grasp and receive this, then the fullness of impartation from the rest of the Priestly Prayer of the Blessing will become available to you!

PRAYER OF DECLARATION

Heavenly Father, I come to You in the name of Yeshua (Jesus). I thank You that You are not indifferent to the hurts, suffering, and attacks of the enemy in my life and the lives of my loved ones and friends. Because of what Your Son, Yeshua, did for me on the cross and through His resurrection, whenever I call upon Your name, You are available to save me and send angels of protection to defeat every scheme of the enemy!

Open my eyes, heavenly Father, to not focus on the darkness around me, but rather to see the glory light of Your presence. Help me remember that behind every cross I face is the resurrection and new adventures. I confess my love for You, Abba Father.

MAY YHWH
KEEP YOU

THE HEBREW WORD FOR *KEEP*

The LORD bless you and keep you.
—NUMBERS 6:24

TODAY WE WILL explore the meaning of the abstract English word *keep*. To fully grasp what G-D intended in this prayer, we must look at the Hebrew word *shamar* and its meaning as concrete, not abstract. Most of us think of the word *keep* when it comes to keeping the commandments or the Word of G-D (Deut. 4:40). We equate the word *keep* with obedience.

G-D's statutes and commandments are our directions to safely navigate this life and obtain the favor and blessings that YHWH has for us. But the Hebrew word *shamar* means so much more than the English word *keep*. In reality it carries the idea of guarding. A Jewish shepherd in the wilderness would build a corral to protect his sheep from predators. He would use stones to fashion a wall and then place thornbushes on top to keep out predators, such as wolves. In this prayer of blessing, YHWH (our heavenly Father) says that He will place a hedge of protection around us, hemming us in with thorns to keep the enemy (predators) from getting to us.

For the last couple of days, we've explored the word *bless* and the picture of YHWH kneeling before you as a good parent who would do anything for you, His spiritual child, desiring to demonstrate His availability to you. I shared with you that G-D your Father is making Himself available to you through this first portion of the divine prayer.

Should you and I ignore Him? Should we just stand and look at Him? No! We are moved to respond in our hearts and humble ourselves, and we fall to our knees so we can receive His invitation. Once we are kneeling with Him, we are positioned to receive His divine embrace. The one true G-D of Israel has come down from His heavenly throne to enfold us with His strong, loving arms.

In this second portion of the divine prayer, picture yourself kneeling (humbled) facing G-D our Father. When it says YHWH will keep you, it is as if He now enfolds you in His arms with a divine embrace.

His arms are likened to a thorny hedge of protection. Satan and his demons can never penetrate the security of the arms of YHWH. You are protected from all things. Why? G-D sees us as His spiritual sons and daughters because of what Yeshua (Jesus) did on the cross (Rom. 8:14–15). When YHWH (your heavenly Father) places His arms around you in His divine embrace, nothing can hurt you or separate you from Him (vv. 31–35). His divine embrace brings security, protection, and victory over the enemy's forces (vv. 37–39).

Satan and his principalities and powers are committed to interfering with us and our G-D-given destiny and purpose! Above all, Satan hates YHWH and doesn't want us to get anywhere close to G-D the Father because he knows we will be given the power and authority to help set spiritual captives free.

With the divine embrace of our heavenly Father through this prayer of blessing, we are delivered instantly from the enemy's attacks—whether it be from others, from spiritual harassment, from oppression, or, in some cases, from possession.

Some have sought deliverance, only to find that even though they gain relief for a short time after the deliverance is performed, most times the attacks begin again. It may not be in the same area they were delivered from before; this time a new area of conflict, oppression, or harassment occurs. It is as if they are continuously consumed by an unending cycle of deliverance as a way of life.

When we pursue deliverance as a way of life, it is almost as if we are not seeking our heavenly Father and His presence. Instead, we are trying to identify the demonic spirit coming against us. YHWH loves you and honors your request when you seek deliverance. But the process sometimes seems never-ending. It might be that we are even empowering the demonic realm by believing that Satan has so much power over us.

Through this second portion of the prayer, when YHWH comes and supernaturally places His arms around you in His divine embrace, you don't have to ask for deliverance—it is done instantly for you.

> The LORD is my pillar, and my fortress, and my deliverer; my [G-D], my rock, in whom I take refuge; my shield, and the horn of my salvation, my high tower.
>
> —PSALM 18:2

Again, I point out that it is OK for you to seek an end to harassment and attacks of the enemy through deliverance from demonic spirits. YHWH will honor those efforts. Better yet, if you allow the impartation of His name (*shem*) to come upon you through this Priestly Prayer of the Blessing, you receive Him (His very person, His holy character, and His power and authority). In this second portion of the divine prayer of the blessing, through G-D's divine embrace, deliverance and protection come without your asking. It is that simple! When you come into an understanding of the full revelation of what this prayer of blessing is accomplishing and imputing to you, it will be life transforming!

Prayer of Declaration

I come before You, heavenly Father, in the name of Yeshua (Jesus), Your only begotten Son. Father, I humble myself before You and desire Your divine embrace. Through this portion of the Priestly Prayer of the Blessing may You enfold me with Your strong arms as a thorny hedge of protection to keep my enemies far way. Even more than protection, I desire to receive Your love and to know You in a far more intimate way. I look forward to this powerful opportunity to experience You, my heavenly Father, in a supernatural, intimate, and experiential way like never before.

THE PSALM 91 CONNECTION

He who dwells in the shelter of the Most High shall abide under the
shadow of the Almighty.

—Psalm 91:1

TODAY WE WILL look at the connection between the prayer of blessing and one of the most well-known psalms about G-D's protection for His people: Psalm 91. I have always found the words of Psalm 91 to be anointed and filled with power to bring divine protection and keep us from harm. When I received the revelation of the divine prayer of blessing in Numbers 6, I suddenly realized that the full impartation of Psalm 91 is related to this second portion of the prayer: "YHWH keep you." This is an impartation of G-D as our protector!

As we see, this well-known psalm begins by directing us to make it our aim to abide in the secret place of YHWH (our heavenly Father). This isn't just an intellectual exercise; YHWH is making Himself available to us, enfolding His strong arms around us—so that His shadow of protection covers us.

For another person's shadow to cover you, you must be very close to that person, and the person must be big. As we delve deeper into the connection between Psalm 91 and this second portion of the prayer of blessing, we begin to understand the powerful revelation of what happens as our heavenly Father enfolds His arms around us in a divine embrace.

I will say of the LORD, "He is my refuge and my fortress, my [G-D] in whom I trust."

—Psalm 91:2

The main point of Psalm 91:2 is that we confess Him as being our place of refuge, our fortress, and it's an admission that we have complete trust in Him. It is one thing to confess that He is your refuge and fortress, but this confession becomes a reality when we realize that He is truly right in front of us. The protection fully comes as we allow Him to enfold us with His strong arms in a divine embrace.

> Surely He shall deliver you from the snare of the hunter and from the deadly pestilence.
>
> —PSALM 91:3

Here is a clear reference that in His arms, in His divine embrace, we will experience His deliverance from the hunter—or, as some translations such as the King James Version say, "the fowler."

What is a fowler? This refers to people who hunt fowl. More specific than just being hunters, they are professional bird hunters. In the days before firearms, birds were captured through an interesting method in which the hunter would take young birds from a nest and raise them by hand. When they had become tame, they were confined in hidden cages so that their voices would call others of their kind, and then the arrows of concealed hunters (fowlers) could kill them.

This scripture refers to being protected from this particular tactic, in which innocent, young, and impressionable people are entrapped by Satan himself "and raised by his hand." Their voices, or the very character of these people, attract others who are of like kind, meaning those who have their same faults or weaknesses. Those who are attracted are then picked off by hunter demons ready to destroy and kill. In the divine embrace of our heavenly Father, we are protected because the enemy cannot come near us under His impenetrable protection.

Likewise, in the divine embrace of G-D, no pestilence can harm you because where YHWH is, there is no sickness! His kingdom is perfect because He is there, and through His divine embrace we are immersed in the atmosphere of heaven.

He shall cover you with His feathers, and under His wings you shall find protection; His faithfulness shall be your shield and wall.

—PSALM 91:4

This directly relates to G-D's arms embracing us like a mother bird to protect us and keep us safe. His faithfulness refers to His promises becoming our shield to deflect any attacks of the enemy's arrows.

You shall not be afraid of the terror by night, nor of the arrow that flies by day; nor of the pestilence that pursues in darkness, nor of the destruction that strikes at noonday.

—PSALM 91:5–6

This passage guarantees that even when we are in the darkness of the night and danger appears to be lurking, we can be reassured because of His divine embrace that we are not alone. He is with us, protecting us.

When we are going through our day, we do not have to be afraid that the enemy can be lurking and even stalking us to do harm. YHWH surrounds us with His thorny arms of protection, which keep the predators from having access to us.

A thousand may fall at your side and ten thousand at your right hand, but it shall not come near you.

—PSALM 91:7

We may be witnessing the insanity of the world around us with people engaged in a battle against one another. The danger of their warfare may bring casualties when we look to our right and left—very close to us—but He promises that His divine embrace will not allow this aimless violence to affect us.

Only with your eyes shall you behold and see the reward of the wicked.

—PSALM 91:8

The New Living Translation translates that verse this way:

Just open your eyes, and see how the wicked are punished.

Being in His divine embrace, we are given eyes to see beyond the apparent prosperity of those who are wicked. We will be given insight to see things through YHWH's own eyes. We will be enabled to see what lies behind the exterior success of those who are wicked. We will no longer envy them because we will see the truth of G-D's justice that will someday be enforced on them. On the outside they may look happy, but those who live apart from Him suffer and grieve on the inside! You can be sure of that!

> Because you have made the LORD, who is my refuge, even the Most High, your dwelling, there shall be no evil befall you, neither shall any plague come near your tent; for He shall give His angels charge over you to guard you in all your ways. They shall bear you up in their hands, lest you strike your foot against a stone.
>
> —PSALM 91:9–12

This passage emphasizes that we are immune to plagues because we have G-D's very name placed on us. We will have angels surrounding us to keep us protected wherever we are and wherever we go. These angels, assigned by YHWH Himself, bear us up to protect us from hitting our foot on a stone.

> You shall tread upon the lion and adder; the young lion and the serpent you shall trample underfoot.
>
> —PSALM 91:13

When we are in His keeping, we will have victory over the predators lurking, watching us, waiting until they determine we are weak, ready to attack us at the time when we appear most vulnerable.

YHWH allows us to see them and where they are hiding. If we choose to go after them, we will be victorious! The lion symbolizes the strongest of our enemies; the adder (serpent) symbolizes those who are stealth and sneaky and can swiftly strike, inflicting a bite that injects us with poison, bringing a slow and painful death.

The serpent also represents Satan himself. Yeshua's victory on the cross treaded on the serpent, and He has Satan's very head under His feet. So too we who are seated in heavenly places with Messiah can step on Satan and impair him from attacking.

> Because he has set his love upon Me, therefore I will deliver him; I will set him on high, because he has known My name.
>
> —Psalm 91:14

That verse reminds us that all the stated promises within Psalm 91 come about by setting our hearts, minds, souls, spirits, and every fiber of our beings on loving the one true G-D of Israel and desiring that He will be first in our lives.

The heavenly Father is telling us that all this is possible because we have known His name. The promised result of the Priestly Prayer of the Blessing being proclaimed over you is that He places His name on you. His *shem* (His very person, His holy character, His power and authority) is imparted and placed on you!

This means He delivers us and sets us high above the enemy and the things of this world. The enemy of our souls cannot harm us. The ultimate promise of YHWH (our heavenly Father) is proclaimed in His own words in the last two verses of Psalm 91.

> He shall call upon Me, and I will answer him; I will be with him in trouble, and I will deliver him and honor him. With long life I will satisfy him and show him My salvation.
>
> —Psalm 91:15–16

The full amplified Hebrew-to-English translation of this portion of the Priestly Prayer of the Blessing is far more than what we find in our Bibles. Our English Bibles say:

The LORD bless you and keep you...

—NUMBERS 6:24

But the amplified Hebrew-to-English translation is:

May YHWH (YeHoVaH, YaHWeH, your heavenly Father) guard you with a hedge of thorny protection that will prevent Satan and all your enemies from harming you. May He protect your body, soul, mind, and spirit, your loved ones, and all your possessions!

When our Jewish High Priest, Yeshua, proclaims this portion of the Priestly Prayer of the Blessing on you, YHWH (your heavenly Father) will appear before you and will give you His divine embrace.

PRAYER OF DECLARATION

I come before You, heavenly Father, in the name of Yeshua (Jesus), Your only begotten Son, my Messiah and Lord (Adonai). I thank You for the revelation through Your Priestly Prayer of the Blessing that when You enfold me in Your strong divine arms, I can access Your Psalm 91 protection.

I am excited that I will soon be experiencing on a daily basis Your divine embrace through this prayer. In Your intimate presence all my needs can be instantly met. In heaven there is no sickness, lack, loneliness, despair, or emotional distress. The enemy cannot enter. In Your divine embrace is the reality of that which is good and perfect. Thank You for this journey of understanding the full meaning and implication of the only prayer You have written in the entire Bible.

SECTION IV

MAY YHWH
SHINE HIS FACE
UPON YOU

THE HEBREW WORD FOR *FACE*

The LORD *bless you and keep you; the* LORD *make His face…*

—NUMBERS 6:24–25

WE'VE DISCUSSED THE words *Lord*, *bless*, and *keep*. Today we will look at the next abstract word in the prayer of blessing: *face*. The Hebrew word *panim* comes from the root *panah*, which means to turn. The word *panim* is plural, and in Hebrew it implies more than one face—not just a happy face but also a sad face, an angry face, and the entire being revealed in the face.

This means when we behold G-D's face, we can see Him as He truly is—fully divine yet a person. When we see Him face to face, we can observe that He has expressions that connote His emotions, thoughts, and judgments. We forget that G-D is a person, and yet the Scriptures are full of illustrations of this fact.

YHWH gets angry.

And the LORD was angry with Solomon because he turned his heart away from the LORD [G-D] of Israel, who had appeared to him twice, and had warned him about this, that he should not follow other gods, but he was disobedient to the LORD's command.

—1 KINGS 11:9–10

YHWH has wrath.

The wrath of [G-D] is revealed from heaven against all ungodliness and unrighteousness of men, who hold the truth in unrighteousness.

—ROMANS 1:18, KJV

YHWH can hate.

> Those who boast will not stand in Your sight; You hate all workers of iniquity.
>
> —Psalm 5:5

I must say that I am very glad I am saved and standing in Yeshua's (Jesus') shadow. G-D has a pure hate, but it is also a complete and just hate. The Father hates sin because it is sin that brings sickness, poverty, divorce, murder, wars, and ultimately death. Yet He loves that which is holy because this is what brings wholeness, completeness, and blessings! I am so thankful that I do not have to face G-D's judgment, but instead, I receive His love and favor!

YHWH takes pleasure in people and things.

> For the Lord takes pleasure in His people; He will beautify the meek with salvation.
>
> —Psalm 149:4

YHWH gets sad and grieves.

> The Lord saw that the wickedness of man was great on the earth, and that every intent of the thoughts of his heart was continually only evil. The Lord was sorry that He had made man on the earth, and it grieved Him in His heart.
>
> —Genesis 6:5–6

YHWH has pity.

> As a father pities his children, so the Lord pities those who fear Him.
>
> —Psalm 103:13, nkjv

YHWH has compassion.

The LORD is gracious and full of compassion, slow to anger, and great in mercy.

—PSALM 145:8

YHWH can be jealous.

You shall not bow down to them, nor serve them. For I, the LORD your [G-D], am a jealous [G-D], visiting the iniquity of the fathers on the children, and on the third and fourth generations of those who hate Me.

—DEUTERONOMY 5:9

So you see that YHWH (our heavenly Father) is a person. G-D sent His only begotten Son, Yeshua, to demonstrate how much He loves us—to demonstrate His holy character. Yeshua is the fullness of the Godhead—the Elohim—in bodily form for us to see. (See Colossians 2:8–10.)

G-D had given us His Word, but mankind didn't comprehend and implement G-D's instruction and precepts. G-D wanted us to know what He was truly like. The compassion to heal and deliver us is what G-D desired to demonstrate to us all along!

G-D the Father is a person, and He desires a relationship with us! He desires to fellowship and commune and exchange intimacy. That's why He went to such lengths pursuing us and sending Yeshua (His only begotten Son) to open the way for us to obtain intimacy! G-D desires a two-way relationship! The precepts and commandments He has given us in His Law (Torah) are perfect. Through instruction and the commandments that Yeshua shared and clarified, our heavenly Father gives us the way to have an intimate relationship with Him.

Many scriptures in the Tanakh (Old Testament) encourage us to seek the face of YHWH. Our heavenly Father desires to have communion with us. The very first commandment is, "Love the LORD your [G-D] with all your heart and mind and with all your soul and with all your strength [your entire being]" (Deut. 6:5, AMP; see also Matt. 22:37; Mark 12:30; Luke 10:27).

The encouragement to seek the face of YHWH (our heavenly Father) alludes to the importance of getting to know the G-D of Israel in the most intimate way.

> When You said, "Seek My face," my heart said to You, "Your face, LORD, I will seek."
>
> —PSALM 27:8

Remember the first portion of the Priestly Prayer of the Blessing? It dealt with the fact that YHWH wants to bless you. YHWH is kneeling before you as a good parent who would do anything for you, His child, desiring to demonstrate His availability to you. As a child seeing your Daddy kneeling in front of you with His arms extended, inviting you, you are moved to respond and humble yourself, and you fall to your knees so you can receive His invitation.

I also shared with you about the second portion of the prayer. Once you are kneeling (humbled) facing YHWH, He now enfolds you in His arms with His divine embrace. He embraces you in His arms, which are likened to a thorny hedge of protection. Satan and his demons can never penetrate the security of the arms of YHWH. You are protected from all things. When your heavenly Father places His arms around you with His divine embrace, nothing can hurt you or separate you from Him.

In the third portion of the Priestly Prayer of the Blessing, which we embarked upon today, your heavenly Father now loosens His embrace. While still keeping His holy hands on your shoulders, He pulls away so you can now see Him face to face.

PRAYER OF DECLARATION

Heavenly Father, I confess now that my desire is to see You face to face. I accept Your invitation for true intimacy. I pray in the name of Yeshua (Jesus) that my desires and decisions line up with all that You have destined for me to pursue. I long to see Your eyes of love and Your smile of approval. I am excited that soon I will hear Your voice as You reveal the purpose and assignments I am to accomplish here on earth on a daily basis. I worship You, Abba Father, and praise Your holy name!

WHY DID MOSES WANT TO
SEE HIS FACE?

The LORD spoke to Moses face to face,
just as a man speaks to his friend.

—Exodus 33:11

IN THE BOOK of Exodus we read that Moses stopped going up Mount Sinai to meet with YHWH. Before the actual tabernacle was erected where YHWH would take up residence in the holy of holies in the form of the Shekinah glory, Moses fashioned a temporary dwelling place where he could meet with YHWH. (See Exodus 33:7–11.)

In that tent of meeting YHWH came to dwell in the form of the Shekinah glory until the tabernacle in the wilderness was built. I must stress this point: the Shekinah glory is not just a thing but a person, the person of YHWH (our heavenly Father) Himself.

I can't imagine what it felt like when Moses stood amid the cloud of the Shekinah glory, which was the manifestation of the actual presence of the Father Himself. Moses could hear YHWH's voice and spoke to Him as a man speaks to another man. Moses saw the bright light—the glory light—inside the cloud, but the cloud obscured the light source.

Yet Moses wanted to see beyond the glory cloud (vv. 18–20). Moses wanted to see the source of the light hidden by the cloud, which Moses referred to as the glory of G-D. But YHWH let Moses know that the glory light in the cloud was His very face (*panim*). Moses couldn't see the *panim* of G-D clearly without the surrounding cloud that hid the full view. Anyone who beheld His face in that way would surely die.

And yet YHWH communicated in the Tanakh (Old Testament) that we are to seek His face. This means if we truly love Him with all our heart, mind, soul, spirit, and strength, we would want to have the highest level of intimacy possible. King David valued this type of intimacy with YHWH.

> Do not hide Your face from me in the day when I am in trouble; incline Your ear to me; in the day when I call answer me quickly.
> —PSALM 102:2

Jacob wrestled with the angel of the Lord, desiring that YHWH would bless him. When he received the blessing of having his name changed from Jacob to Israel (the father of the twelve sons who led the twelve tribes of Israel), he recognized that he had seen the very face (*panim*) of YHWH in the person of the angel of the Lord.

> Jacob called the name of the place Peniel, saying, "I have seen [G-D] face to face, and my life has been preserved."
> —GENESIS 32:30

Yeshua was the face of the Father when He was on earth. Even when we were still in our sinful state, to look at Jesus was to behold the very face of YHWH (our heavenly Father). Yet instead of bringing death, peering into the face of Yeshua brought us salvation and life everlasting! The Scriptures contain a powerful example concerning this truth in Luke 7.

Yeshua's parable in this passage points out that He came to reach the brokenhearted—not the self-righteous—because they truly needed salvation and as a result of receiving their miracle would begin to love G-D with all their heart, mind, soul, spirit, and strength. Yet the most significant portion of this account is what happened next.

> Then He turned to the woman and said to Simon, "Do you see this woman? I entered your house. You gave Me no water for My feet, but she has washed My feet with her tears and wiped them with the

hair of her head. You gave Me no kiss, but this woman, since the time I came in, has not ceased to kiss My feet. You did not anoint My head with oil, but this woman has anointed My feet with ointment. Therefore I say to you, her sins, which are many, are forgiven, for she loved much. But he who is forgiven little loves little."

Then He said to her, "Your sins are forgiven."

—LUKE 7:44–48

This woman of ill repute was afraid to look up at the face of Yeshua, but she had likely been affected by hearing His words or by the miracles He had performed. Yeshua turned to the woman and addressed her face to face. She looked into the eyes of Yeshua as He talked directly to her for the first time.

Remember, YHWH told Moses in Exodus that he could never see G-D's face, or he would surely die. Yeshua (the only begotten Son of G-D) represented His Father on earth. When this woman of ill repute looked into the face of Yeshua, she was beholding the very face of G-D the Father. Instead of receiving death, she received life, deliverance, healing, and transformation.

How did she receive them? She received them by gazing into the beatific face (*panim*) of Yeshua and hearing His comforting words as she watched them being formed from His lips.

In summary, in the Tanakh (Old Covenant), G-D kept Moses from seeing His face because of the stain of original sin. In the new covenant Yeshua was the face of the living G-D, made flesh and walking among us (John 1:14). When you looked into Yeshua's eyes, you were looking into the face of G-D!

For in [Yeshua] lives all the fullness of the Godhead [Elohim] bodily.

—COLOSSIANS 2:9

Today we who are believers in Messiah are called to be the face of G-D for others to see! Believers today can accept that we can approach YHWH (our heavenly Father) through His only begotten Son, Yeshua.

But there's more! YHWH is not only making His face accessible to you. Tomorrow we will dig deep into what it means for Him to make His face shine on you.

PRAYER OF DECLARATION

Heavenly Father, I come before You in the name of Yeshua (Jesus). Like Moses, the cry of my heart is, "I want to see Your face!" I now understand that under the old covenant no one could see Your face and live. But under the new covenant, Yeshua's blood has cleansed me. Second Corinthians 5:21 says, "[G-D] made Him [Yeshua] who knew no sin to be sin for us, that we might become the righteousness of [G-D the Father] in Him [Yeshua]."

Yeshua (Jesus) made the way possible so I can now boldly enter the heavenly throne room and seek Your face. I realize that one encounter with You, face to face, can forever change my life. Thank You, Yeshua (Jesus), for making the way possible to see my heavenly Father face to face.

Yeshua is the way, the truth, and the life. No one can come to know You, the one true G-D, as Father except through Him.

THE HEBREW WORD FOR *SHINE*

The LORD bless you and keep you; the LORD make His face to shine upon you.

—NUMBERS 6:24–25

NOW THAT WE are halfway through our thirty-day journey, let's recap. In the first portion of the Priestly Prayer of the Blessing, YHWH (your heavenly Father) kneels in front of you, His spiritual son or daughter, as a good parent desiring to make Himself available and minister to you. In the second portion, your heavenly Father places His arms around you with a divine embrace, holding you in His strong arms of protection and security. In the third portion, it's as if He loosens His divine embrace, and while still keeping His holy hands on your shoulders, He pulls away enough for you to see Him face to face so you can experience His reality and person.

We will now explore what it means for YHWH (your heavenly Father) to make His face shine on you! To get started, we need to understand that Hebraic thought equates light to order and darkness to chaos.

In the beginning [G-D] created the heavens and the earth. The earth was formless and void, darkness [chaos] was over the surface of the deep, and the Spirit of [G-D] was moving over the surface of the water. [G-D] said, "Let there be light [order]," and there was light [order]. [G-D] saw that the light [order] was good, and [G-D] separated the light [order] from the darkness [chaos].

—GENESIS 1:1–4

By amplifying those verses with this concept, we see chaos when the earth was without form, void, and in the dark. Light had to be created first so that YHWH could bring order. When the prayer of blessing is proclaimed over you by Yeshua (Jesus) our High Priest, you will find that the face of G-D shining on you brings order. As the Father imparts a portion of Himself on you, your thoughts will become singular.

The enemy of our souls loves to bring confusion. As the enemy attacks us with circumstances, trials, and challenges, we often find ourselves embroiled in conflicting thoughts. We often become apprehensive and disquieted, and sometimes this leads to oppression or even depression. Many times we are conflicted and puzzled when making decisions.

Yet when the face of YHWH (our heavenly Father) begins to shine on us, we sense that everything will be OK. Suddenly we become single-minded. Our thoughts become aligned with His thoughts.

Just as YHWH said at creation, "Let there be light," to bring to order what was in darkness and chaos, so too this occurs when we can spiritually see His face (*panim*) because His face is the source of illumination—of light. *Or* is the Hebrew word for *shine*, and it connotes that when the light of His face begins to shine on you, He brings order into your life. Chaos, wrong thinking, and conflicting thoughts must leave. Your G-D-given purpose, your calling, becomes crystal clear. You suddenly begin to understand the revelation of a step-by-step process that will help you begin to fulfill whatever your G-D-given assignment on earth truly is.

Confusion is gone, conflicting thoughts are gone, and the enemy's interference is negated. Now YHWH is ready to begin His creation, His restoration, His breathing new life into you so that you can move to the next level of His glory.

The Hebrew word for *restoration* is *arukah*. "The biblical meaning of the word 'restoration' is to receive back more than has been lost to the point that the final state is greater than the original condition....

Unlike the regular dictionary's meaning of 'restoration,' which is to return something to its original condition, the biblical definition of the word has greater connotations that go above and beyond the typical everyday usage."[1]

When the face of YHWH (your heavenly Father) radiates the glory light of His presence toward you, things are transformed. The children of Israel became slaves in Egypt by a wicked taskmaster, Pharaoh. G-D appeared to Moses in the burning bush in the wilderness. It was the light of His very person in that bush, and Moses heard the voice of G-D projecting out from the light of G-D's face shining on him.

Moses received clear instructions. He was tasked with being G-D's chosen vessel to deliver the Israelites out of bondage. More than His delivering them out of the hands of Pharaoh, YHWH wanted to impart a covenant relationship with them where He (YHWH) would call them into order. He did this through imparting His Torah (His instructions, precepts, and commandments) so they could thrive even in the desert.

In Exodus 23, G-D promises seven specific blessings to those who walk in His precepts and fellowship with Him during His weekly Sabbath and in His appointed times, the seven feasts of YHWH.

1. He will send an angel before you to guard you.
2. He will be an enemy to your enemies.
3. He will bless you with provision.
4. He will remove sickness from you.
5. There will be no miscarrying or barrenness among you.
6. He will fulfill the number of your days, and you will not die early.
7. You will become fruitful and take possession of the land.

Then again, YHWH appeared to Moses on Mount Sinai in the form of the Shekinah glory, His very face beaming and causing Moses' face to shine with the reflection of G-D's glory. Amid the glory is where YHWH gave Moses the Ten Commandments, written by His own finger. You see, the greatest communication comes when we are close to the face of G-D our Father shining on us!

Moses then spent time with G-D in the temporary dwelling place, the tent of meeting, standing in the Shekinah glory. It was there in the glory where the one true G-D imparted to Moses His precepts and instruction as contained in the Torah. All this was given to bring order to the chaos Satan had wrought on the earth, deceiving even the very elite since the fall of Adam and Eve.

After Moses received the Ten Commandments, YHWH gave Moses the Priestly Prayer of the Blessing. When this portion of the divine prayer is proclaimed over you in the name (*shem*) of Yeshua, the Jewish High Priest in heaven, the very face of your heavenly Father will shine on you as it did on Moses. The face of Moses began to shine from the reflection of being in the presence of the Shekinah glory—the illumination of the very face (*panim*) of G-D shining out from the cloud toward him.

The impartation of the words of the Torah came to Moses while spending time in the Shekinah glory of the Most High G-D. Enlightenment comes to us, opening understanding from the Word of G-D, which proceeds out of the face of our heavenly Father illuminating His revelation on us.

When YHWH appears before you face to face as a result of this portion of the Priestly Prayer of the Blessing, His face shines on you. His mouth proceeds to declare words of blessing and promises that come alive as they ignite and bear fruit in your life! Darkness is dispelled.

The Hebrew word *or* also speaks of a door, or a portal. Order opens the door to the next level, to the next opportunity, and into the supernatural of G-D. When the face of your heavenly Father shines on you, a doorway, or portal, to heaven opens. When the face of YHWH comes close to you and you gaze into His loving eyes, you begin to see heavenly things.

PRAYER OF DECLARATION

Heavenly Father, I ask in the name of Yeshua (Jesus) that You begin to shine Your face upon me. I need You to bring order into my life. I pray that You will expel any darkness and confusion in me and around me. I desire to be single-minded and have my every thought aligned with Yours. May chaos, wrong thinking, and conflicting ideas leave. Let Your face shine upon me so that I clearly understand Your assignments so I can begin to fulfill Your purpose and calling for my life here on earth. I thank You for guiding me step-by-step on Your pathway to righteousness and fulfillment.

DOORWAYS TO HEAVEN

How awesome is this place! This is none other but the house of [G-D], and this is the gate of heaven.

—GENESIS 28:17

OORWAYS, OR PORTALS, into heaven are talked about in the Tanakh (Old Testament). Before G-D's covenant with Moses and the children of Israel, these portals were avenues where angels could ascend and descend and certain individuals could get a glimpse of what was in heaven.

Jacob, whose name was changed by G-D to Israel, discovered a heavenly portal. Jacob spent the night in a place where his grandfather Abraham had "called upon the name of the LORD" (Gen. 13:4). Jacob fell asleep with his head propped up on a "covenant stone." His dream was so real that it transformed his life. (See Genesis 28:11–17.)

A portal opened for Jacob, which was a way he could glimpse into heaven and see YHWH in the form of His Shekinah glory. In addition, he received a word that echoed the same promises concerning the land of Israel as an inheritance that YHWH gave to his father, Isaac, and his grandfather Abraham. Jacob made a pillar out of the stone on which he had laid his head. Jacob called it the "Dwelling Place of YHWH (YeHoVaH or YaHWeH)."

Ezekiel experienced an even greater portal, or door, into heaven, which opened to him during the Israelites' Babylonian captivity in Ezekiel 1:1; 3:22–23. Not only did he see into heaven and behold the Shekinah glory of YHWH (YeHoVaH or YaHWeH), but he experienced the impartation of the power of the glory as it emitted from the face of G-D shining down on him.

King David, under the inspiration of the Ruach HaKodesh (Holy Spirit), wrote about the appearance of YHWH in the glory as He comes through such a door, or portal.

> Lift up your heads, O you gates [portals]; and be lifted up, you everlasting doors, that the King of glory may enter. Who is this King of glory? [YHWH] strong and mighty, [YHWH] mighty in battle.
>
> —PSALM 24:7–8

YESHUA, OUR DOORWAY

Yeshua said that He was the only way to heaven, whereby we have access to YHWH (John 10:9; 14:6). Yeshua alluded to being the "Door of the Tabernacle." There was only one way to go into the tabernacle (a type or foreshadowing of the heavenly tabernacle). Yeshua was saying that He was that door!

Yeshua opened a portal, or a door, by which we can now have access to the Father. We can, by faith, go into the holy of holies in heaven (G-D's throne room), where Yeshua is seated at the right hand of the Father, Yeshua's throne being the heavenly mercy seat.

> Let us then come with confidence to the throne of grace, that we may obtain mercy and find grace to help in time of need.
>
> —HEBREWS 4:16

When this portion of the divine prayer is pronounced over you in the name of Yeshua, your High Priest, you do not have to go up by faith into the heavenly throne room, but rather the face of YHWH (your heavenly Father) comes down from heaven to shine on you.

Paul shares how the end of our journey is ultimately seeing G-D face to face. Our spiritual journey on earth is likened to looking in a mirror and beholding the reflection of YHWH (our heavenly Father).

When I was a child, I spoke as a child, I understood as a child, and I thought as a child. But when I became a man, I put away childish things. For now we see as through a glass, dimly, but then, face to face. Now I know in part, but then I shall know, even as I also am known.

—1 CORINTHIANS 13:11–12

Of course, the fullness of seeing G-D our Father face to face will occur after the resurrection, when our bodies are instantly changed from what is corruptible to what is immortal! At that time, we won't just be G-D's spiritual sons and daughters; we will be G-D's physical children.

Yet we need to know that during this end-time preparation for Yeshua's return, when New Jerusalem descends from heaven to earth, through the rediscovery of the prayer of blessing we can begin to have G-D's face (*panim*) shining His glory on us! When this happens, it will usher us into being transformed from one level of glory to the next.

Nevertheless when anyone turns to the Lord, the veil is removed. Now the Lord is the Spirit. And where the Spirit of the Lord is, there is liberty. But we all, seeing the glory of [YHWH] with unveiled faces, as in a mirror, are being transformed into the same image from glory to glory by the Spirit of the Lord.

—2 CORINTHIANS 3:16–18

PRAYER OF DECLARATION

Heavenly Father, I come to You longing for a face-to-face encounter with You. I do not want to remain spiritually stagnant. In the name of Yeshua (Jesus), I ask that You shine Your face upon me so that I might begin to move from one level of Your glory to the next.

Remove any scales from my eyes so I can clearly see into the supernatural and behold Your glorious face. May the atmosphere of heaven overwhelm me and transform me so that all who come in contact with me will sense Your glory upon me, within me, and flowing out of me to them. I pray this in the name of Yeshua (Jesus).

THE FACE OF YHWH IS SHINING UPON YOU

*Finally, brothers, whatever things are true, whatever
things are honest, whatever things are just, whatever things
are pure, whatever things are lovely, whatever things are of
good report, if there is any virtue, and if there is
any praise, think on these things.*

—Philippians 4:8

Today we will continue to deepen our understanding of the Hebrew word for *shine*. When YHWH (our heavenly Father) shines His face (*panim*) on you, His order is imparted to you and your thoughts become His thoughts. When the face of G-D shines on you, you won't have to strive to place your mind in subjection to meditate on such thoughts. It's not you having to try to take every thought captive to obtain the "mind of Messiah."

> For the weapons of our warfare are not of the flesh but have divine power to destroy strongholds. We destroy arguments and every lofty opinion raised against the knowledge of [YHWH], and take every thought captive to obey [Messiah].
>
> —2 Corinthians 10:4–5, esv

By being in such intimacy with our heavenly Father, you receive divine thinking that overpowers your thoughts and human reasoning with His perfect and pure thoughts! An outpouring of His grace transfers to you through the illumination of His glory.

THE SHINING FACE OF G-D IMPARTS REVELATION

We receive instruction from the face of G-D. His mouth whispers words when He is close to us. His Word is a lamp to our feet—it lights the way, the path, the narrow road that we should follow.

> Your word is a lamp to my feet and a light to my path.
>
> —PSALM 119:105

It's not a struggle when we are in His presence. We become centered, not wanting to go to the left or the right without His instruction or beckoning. Sometimes He is directing us to retreat! Other times He gently compels us to stay perfectly still, waiting and basking in Him as He appears to us in the form of the Shekinah glory. We are to wait so we can be replenished, strengthened, invigorated, and bathed in heavenly downloads of His instruction and His revelation.

> But those who wait upon the LORD shall renew their strength; they shall mount up with wings as eagles, they shall run and not be weary, and they shall walk and not faint.
>
> —ISAIAH 40:31

Since that day, my life has never been the same. As I proclaim the Priestly Prayer of the Blessing over myself in the manner in which YHWH instructed, in the name (*shem*) of Yeshua my High Priest—I find myself more in sync moment by moment each day with the one true G-D of Israel's plans for my life.

It is normal for me to be in constant communication with the Father even when I'm doing minimal tasks, when I'm watching the news on TV, when I'm driving in my car, or when people are talking to me. I sense Him helping me filter the conversation in light of eternity. My level of discernment has been sharpened.

The Book of Hebrews declares that mature religion has your senses exercised to discern both good and evil.

> But solid food belongs to those who are of full age [spiritually mature], that is, those who by reason of use have their senses exercised to discern both good and evil.
>
> —HEBREWS 5:14, NKJV

When the Father's face comes close to you, you begin to see through His eyes and hear through His ears. You begin to smell whether the atmosphere is of G-D or the enemy. Your heart becomes filled with the things of G-D and eternity—you become full of compassion. Your mind is no longer conflicted, having to cast down ungodly imaginations, fleshly temptations, evil, or accusations of the enemy. Instead, your mind is filled with those things that are good, lovely, and of good report (Phil. 4:8).

Each day when I proclaim the Priestly Prayer of the Blessing over myself, I find that He and His Ruach HaKodesh (Holy Spirit) become stronger in me. I am enabled to function at a higher level with all the responsibilities I have, first as a husband, father, and grandfather and with all the many tasks I have to perform in my job and ministry.

Many people who daily work alongside me ask me how I can accomplish so much. I believe that all glory must go to G-D for revealing Yeshua's reality as my Messiah and Lord (Adonai) when I received the new birth and placing the Ruach HaKodesh (Holy Spirit) within me and on me. Yet greatest of all is the Father making Himself known to me tangibly.

For me, it began with YHWH (the heavenly Father) revealing Himself to me in a dream I had as a little boy. I know now that my main purpose for being born is to share the revelation that you can enter a life guided by the power of the Most High G-D through this prayer of blessing.

It is one thing to be successful, but many times our achievements can be built on the "dead bodies" of others! I'm moved when others tell me they have observed my attitude as being "full of peace, gentleness, and humility." When conflicts arise and the pressures from deadlines come, even amid the enemy's attacks I have been able to exhibit the "fruit of the Ruach HaKodesh." This is not to my credit at all; it is because I have been given access to the Father Himself, along with intimacy with Yeshua and Ruach HaKodesh.

When the face of YHWH is close to you, His voice is released in whispers—the still, small voice of the Lord G-D Almighty is constantly communicating to His spiritual sons and daughters.

In our English Bibles we read this portion stated as:

The LORD make His face to shine upon you.

—NUMBERS 6:25

But in the amplified Hebrew-to-English translation it is:

May YHWH (YeHoVaH, YaHWeH, your heavenly Father) illuminate the wholeness of His being toward you, continually bringing order, so that you will fulfill your G-D-given destiny and purpose.

PRAYER OF DECLARATION

Heavenly Father, I pray in the name of Yeshua (Jesus) that You will begin to shine Your face upon me so that Your divine thoughts overpower my human reasoning. Let Your holy and perfect thoughts illuminate my being. May I experience being face to face with You so I can hear Your words of direction and wisdom.

Let the glory from Your shining face be like a lamp lighting the path I walk upon every day. May I sense Your constant communication and guidance from You when I'm performing minimal tasks driving in my car, and even when others are talking to me. Help me begin to see things through Your eyes and hear things through Your ears. I pray for You to impart to me Your peace, gentleness, and mercy.

SECTION V

MAY YHWH BE
GRACIOUS
TO YOU

THE HEBREW WORD FOR *GRACIOUS*

The LORD make His face to shine upon you,
and be gracious unto you.

—NUMBERS 6:25

W HAT DOES IT mean for G-D to be gracious to you when YHWH's face is shining on you? The Hebrew word for *gracious* is *chanan*, which means to show unmerited favor. Other meanings are to exhibit a yearning toward, demonstrate a longing for, be merciful to, exhibit compassion, be inclined toward, be considerate of, and demonstrate a desire to spare.

When we reflect on G-D's gracious demonstration to the Israelites in the desert, we can better appreciate what our heavenly Father will demonstrate to us when we see Him face to face. Today we'll look at this account from Scripture to deepen our understanding of the Hebrew word for *gracious*.

The children of Israel in the wilderness had witnessed the Egyptians humbled by ten horrible plagues. Yet YHWH didn't harm any of them.

+ They were delivered from the slavery of an evil taskmaster—
  the Pharaoh of Egypt. The hand of YHWH rescued them.
+ They beheld YHWH's pillar of fire keeping the mighty
  army of Egypt at bay.
+ They marveled at the power of YHWH as the Red Sea
  was parted.
+ They watched as the Egyptian army was destroyed before
  their eyes as the waters fell on them.
+ They beheld the cloud of the Shekinah glory and the thun-
  dering of YHWH's voice from Mount Sinai.

Even though they had witnessed the mighty power and benevolence of their G-D, they became frightened, not knowing whether Moses was coming back since he had been gone for forty days and nights. While Moses was away on Mount Sinai meeting with G-D, the children of Israel persuaded Aaron, who would become the high priest, to build them a golden calf to worship in place of the one true G-D of Israel.

Moses was receiving the Ten Commandments, written by YHWH's own finger. The first commandment reads:

> You shall have no other gods before Me. You shall not make for yourself any graven idol, or any likeness of anything that is in heaven above, or that is in the earth beneath, or that is in the water below the earth.
>
> —Exodus 20:3–4

Aaron took from the Israelites the spoils of Egypt and fashioned them into a false god, a golden calf. Aaron had used the gold and silver that was earmarked to build the tabernacle in the wilderness, where the one true G-D would come and dwell inside the holy of holies in the form of the Shekinah glory.

> So they rose up early on the next day, and offered burnt offerings, and brought peace offerings. And the people sat down to eat and to drink, and rose up to play.
>
> —Exodus 32:6

> [YHWH] spoke to Moses, "Go, and get down, for your people, whom you brought out of the land of Egypt, have corrupted themselves....Now therefore let Me alone, so that My wrath may burn against them and I may destroy them. And I will make of you a great nation."
>
> —Exodus 32:7, 10

But Moses reminded YHWH that the children of Israel were G-D's chosen people and that He had made promises to Abraham, Isaac, and Jacob that were everlasting covenants whereby their seed would inherit the land forever. Moses pleaded with G-D and said that it would look bad if He delivered them from the Pharaoh's hand only to consume them in the wilderness—and G-D heard Moses!

[YHWH] relented of the harm which He said He would do to His people.

—EXODUS 32:14

This was true grace. Even when they were disobedient, G-D continued to bless them. YHWH created the Priestly Prayer of the Blessing for the children of Israel so that He might place His name (*shem*) on them. This same prayer is available today, allowing us to walk in G-D's very person, His holy character, and His power and authority.

PRAYER OF DECLARATION

Heavenly Father, I pray in the name of Yeshua (Jesus) that You manifest Your grace upon me as I meet with You face to face through the Priestly Prayer of the Blessing. I desire that You show me Your unmerited favor. I pray for Your demonstration of mercy and compassion, even in times when I feel I have been a disappointment to You. Remove from me any unhealthy fear. Replace fear with a desire to run toward You instead of running away and hiding from You. Help me realize that as my heavenly Father, You will forgive me, heal me, and cause me to be restored. May I experience an impartation of Your shining glory to keep me from pursuing a golden calf as the children of Israel did. I declare that my heart will always desire Your real presence and not a substitution.

THE FATHER HEART OF G-D

But You, O Lord, are...gracious, slow to anger,
and abundant in mercy and truth.

—PSALM 86:15, NKJV

A S BELIEVERS, WE can understand that Yeshua (Jesus) demonstrated those qualities time and time again. Yet we aren't as quick to realize that Yeshua was demonstrating the Father heart of G-D.

Today, as we explore the divine prayer of blessing, we will focus on G-D imparting these things to us through the illumination of His very face as He looks into our eyes and we look back into His. Through the new birth He has become our Father—our Daddy—but we don't comprehend with our natural minds how much He loves us. We can never experience a greater or purer love.

When Yeshua began His ministry, He was fully immersed in the *mikvah* (baptism) by John the Baptist. Yeshua went fully under the water of the Jordan River. When He emerged, the Shekinah glory of YHWH began to shine on Him. It was the glory of the face of YHWH smiling and beaming His love and acceptance.

> And when [Yeshua] was baptized [fully immersed], He came up immediately out of the water. And suddenly the heavens were opened to Him [a door opened], and He saw the [Ruach HaKodesh] descending on Him like a dove. And a voice came from heaven, saying, "This is My beloved Son, in whom I am well pleased."
> —MATTHEW 3:16–17

This was YHWH (the heavenly Father) giving His graciousness—in Hebrew, His *chanan*. It's not just what was said to Yeshua. The truth is Yeshua could sense the love and approval of His Father.

Through the new birth YHWH is our heavenly Father. When our heavenly Father shines His face (*panim*) on us, not only is He imparting order, destiny, and purpose, but He is also showing forth His love and approval. If you and I could see His loving, compassionate eyes as this portion of the divine prayer is proclaimed over us, we would melt and weep uncontrollably. We can never experience a greater love than this.

YHWH (your heavenly Father) is saying to you the same thing He did to Yeshua, His only begotten Son: "You are My beloved son or daughter, in whom I am well pleased." YHWH looks past your shortcomings, your failures, and your weaknesses, and through G-D's divine prayer of grace—the only prayer in the entire Bible written by Him—He makes His face shine on you so you will know His love in the greatest way possible. He is bringing His reassurance: "You are My beloved spiritual son or daughter. I love you."

THE AMPLIFIED HEBREW-TO-ENGLISH MEANING

Other root words derived from the Hebrew word *chanan* mean that G-D will be gracious, providing love, sustenance, and friendship. It is favor far beyond what we deserve. In our English Bibles we read:

> The LORD make His face to shine upon you, and be gracious unto you.
> —NUMBERS 6:25

With the Hebrew meaning in mind, the amplified Hebrew-to-English translation is this:

> May YHWH [YeHoVaH, YaHWeH, your heavenly Father] pro-
> vide you with perfect love and fellowship [never leaving you] and give
> you sustenance [provision] and friendship.

Now, let's review.

"YHWH *blesses* you." In the first portion of the Priestly Prayer of the Blessing, YHWH kneels in front of you, His spiritual son or daughter, as a good parent desiring to make Himself available and minister to you.

"YHWH *keeps* you." In this second portion, YHWH places His arms around you with a divine embrace, holding you in His strong arms of protection and security.

"YHWH makes His *face* to come into view before you." In this portion of the prayer, it's as if He loosens His divine embrace, and while still keeping His holy hands on your shoulders, He pulls away enough for you to see Him face to face so you can begin to experience His reality and person.

Then "YHWH makes His face to *shine* upon you!" In this portion of the Priestly Prayer of the Blessing, YHWH (your heavenly Father) reveals His perfect love to you as your Daddy with loving eyes and a beatific smile. He looks past your weaknesses and your frailties, pledging that He will never leave you and that He will provide you with His love and fellowship and friendship.

It is your heavenly Father saying to you, "You are My beloved son or daughter, in whom I am well pleased." It is an impartation where you will know that you are never alone and He is for you and not against you. The Bible puts it this way:

> For I am persuaded that neither death nor life, neither angels nor principalities nor powers, neither things present nor things to come, neither height nor depth, nor any other created thing, shall be able to separate us from the love of [YHWH], which is in [Messiah Yeshua] our Lord [Adonai].
>
> —ROMANS 8:38–39

PRAYER OF DECLARATION

Heavenly Father, thank You for sending Your only begotten Son, Yeshua, to make the way through which I can become Your spiritual son or daughter. As I begin to experience Your presence through gazing into Your shining face, may I see in Your eyes Your pure love for me. Help me connect with Your heart for me. Help me understand that You choose to look beyond my shortcomings, my failures, and my weaknesses.

May I hear You say, "You are My beloved child, in whom I am well pleased." I love You, Abba Father. I pray all these things in the name of Your only begotten Son, Yeshua (Jesus).

MAY YHWH LIFT HIS COUNTENANCE UPON YOU

THE HEBREW WORD FOR *LIFT*

The LORD lift His countenance upon you.

—NUMBERS 6:26

Today we'll take a closer look at the Hebrew word for *lift*. The Hebrew word *nasa*, which is translated in our English Bibles as the word *lift*, literally means to lift, carry, or take. When this portion of the Priestly Prayer of the Blessing is pronounced over you in the name of Yeshua, our High Priest, your heavenly Father begins to lift you in His strong arms and carry you. When you are lifted up, nothing can harm you, but more importantly, YHWH is imparting Himself to you, transferring everything He is and has for you as your loving Daddy.

Many scriptures in the Tanakh (Old Testament) convey the concept of our heavenly Father lifting and carrying us.

> He delivers me from my enemies. You [YHWH] lift me up above those who rise up against me; You have delivered me from the violent man.
>
> —PSALM 18:48

This scripture says YHWH lifted the Israelites through their journeys. You can apply this same scripture to your own life. He will lift you in His strong, loving arms to deliver you from your enemies, and He will give you divine protection from those who rise against you! This alludes to those who may be close to you but rise against you to do you harm.

Here is another great scripture that talks about our heavenly Father lifting us:

For in the time of trouble [YHWH] will hide me in His pavilion; in the shelter of His tabernacle He will hide me; He will set me up on a rock. Now my head will be lifted up above my enemies encircling me; therefore I will offer sacrifices of joy in His tabernacle; I will sing, yes, I will sing praises to the LORD.

—PSALM 27:5–6

This scripture conveys how YHWH will lift us in His strong arms. He will protect us in our times of trouble and hide us in His pavilion (His dwelling place). He will transport us into the shelter of the Most High (the "secret place," the heavenly holy of holies), hidden and set high on a rock (Yeshua), lifted above every enemy, including Satan and his minions.

Having your head lifted above your enemies means that all who desire to harm you shall know that you are favored by the one true G-D, YHWH. This is further signified in the scripture from the Brit Hadashah (New Testament).

And He raised us up and seated us together in the heavenly places in [Messiah Yeshua], so that in the coming ages [YHWH] might show the surpassing riches of His grace in kindness toward us in [Messiah Yeshua].

—EPHESIANS 2:6–7

Your response is to humble yourself and offer yourself to your heavenly Daddy as He carries you. You respond with joy and sing praises to His name (His very person). Even when you face the most hopeless situation, G-D will lift you up.

Be gracious to me, O LORD; consider my trouble from those who hate me, O You who lifts me up from the gates of death.

—PSALM 9:13

Even when you face death itself, He will be the One who lifts you and delivers you. He truly views you as His son or daughter.

Then I said to you, "Do not be terrified, or afraid of them. [YHWH] who goes before you, He shall fight for you, just as all that He did for you in Egypt before your eyes, and in the wilderness, where you saw how the Lord your [G-D] carried you, as a man carries his son, in all the way that you went, until you came to this place."

—Deuteronomy 1:29–31

You should not be terrified or fear those who are against you and against G-D. Even the Israelites, who were disobedient, were protected by YHWH when they were in the wilderness; G-D carried them "as a man carries his son." His carrying you is a statement that you are His eternal inheritance (Eph. 2:6–7). It's comforting to know how your heavenly Father views you, no matter how young or old you are.

Listen to Me [YHWH], O house of Jacob, and all the remnant of the house of Israel, who are borne by Me from birth and are carried from the womb: and even to your old age I am He, and even to your graying years I will carry you; I have done it, and I will bear you; even I will carry, and will deliver you.

—Isaiah 46:3–4

G-D views you as a child even when you become old and gray. He still carries you in His divine arms without fail. Your heavenly Father carried you when you were in your mother's womb and knew who you would be before the foundation of the world (Eph. 1:3–6).

What does your heavenly Father do as He holds you up in His arms and walks with you? The picture is likened to what a good Father would do when carrying his newborn son or daughter in his arms.

[YHWH] your [G-D] in your midst, the Mighty One, will save; He will rejoice over you with gladness, He will quiet you with His love, He will rejoice over you with singing.

—Zephaniah 3:17, nkjv

Can you envision your heavenly Father walking with you, carrying you in His arms, singing over you, and perhaps dancing?

+ He saves you by lifting you and carrying you in His arms.
+ He openly rejoices over you with gladness. Imagine His saying over you wonderful and uplifting words, renewing you with His words of love.
+ He will quiet you with His words of love. This alludes to a father comforting his child who is crying. Your heavenly Father wants to comfort you in times of distress, kissing you on the forehead and your cheeks, emoting His love and empathy toward you.
+ He will rejoice over you with singing. This is a beautiful image of the Father's intimacy with you.

I remember when my two children, Tara and Joseph, were babies. I carried them in my arms on a pillow. They would look up at me as I quietly spoke words expressing my deep love. I would sing Scripture songs over them. Both of them would begin to smile and try to make sounds. They could sense the love I had for them. When I carried them and we gazed deep into each other's faces, there was no one in the world except my child and me. They had all my attention. This is what your heavenly Father desires to do with you as a result of this portion of the divine prayer.

PRAYER OF DECLARATION

Heavenly Father, thank You that when I feel alone, isolated, or harassed by my enemies, through this portion of Your Priestly Prayer of the Blessing, You promise to rescue me. You desire to lift me up and carry me in Your strong arms of safety. You lift me high above those who have risen against me. My enemies can see that I am favored and loved by You.

You view me as Your child even when I become old and gray. As You carry me, You are rejoicing over me with gladness. You comfort me with fatherly love. You kiss my forehead and my cheeks, and wipe my tears away when I am disquieted. You rejoice over me with singing. In the name of Yeshua (Jesus), let me never forget that You desire to lift me up, walk with me, and gaze deeply into my eyes. I look back at Your radiant face, knowing that You are the author and finisher of my faith.

DAY 22

THE FATHER LIFTS US UP

He delivers me from my enemies. You also lift me up above those who rise against me.

—2 SAMUEL 22:49, NKJV

SINCE I WROTE my book *The Priestly Prayer of the Blessing*, I received a deeper download on the Hebrew word *nasa*, meaning *lift*, from the portion of the prayer that talks about YHWH lifting us. There are many more references in the Word of G-D about the powerful outcome as a result of the Father's desire to rescue us!

> He brought me up out of the pit of destruction, out of the mud; and He set my feet on a rock making my footsteps firm.
>
> —PSALM 40:2, NASB

This verse points to when we are at the lowest point of our lives, stuck in a place likened to quicksand, our heavenly Father lifts us up and places our feet on a rock, making our footsteps firm again. That's why the pronouncing of the Priestly Prayer over us every day is so important. We might be in a hopeless situation, but the heart of our heavenly Father is to place us back on His path of righteousness.

> He raises the poor from the dust, He lifts the needy from the garbage heap to seat them with nobles, and He gives them a seat of honor as an inheritance; for the pillars of the earth are the LORD's, and He set the world on them.
>
> —1 SAMUEL 2:8, NASB

The Father can take us from a place of poverty, when we are filthy and even searching for food in the garbage dump. When YHWH lifts us up with His strong hand, He places us in the seat of honor.

We will feel as if we are dreaming. "How can this be? I was a loser but now I am a victor." The reason is that the Father created the foundations of the earth, and all the riches of the world are His to give to whom He may.

> The LORD supports all who fall, and raises up all who are bowed down.
>
> —Psalm 145:14, nasb

The key to that verse is that we walk in humility. We are bowed down worshipping YHWH, knowing that He will sustain us and lift us up even when we fall.

> You who have shown me many troubles and distresses will revive me again, and will bring me up again from the depths of the earth.
>
> —Psalm 71:20, nasb

Others may think we have one foot in the grave and we are ready to be lowered into that grave. We are to exist with the mindset that His hand is readily extended to lift us up. The result is revival—life from the dead!

When someone we love dies, there is no more hope. We may have been praying for our loved one's healing, but all faith leaves us when we stand in front of a casket.

Imagine how Martha felt when she sent a message to Yeshua (Jesus) that her brother, Lazarus, was dying. By the time Yeshua came, Lazarus had died and had been buried in a tomb for days. She was in total despair. I have often thought, "How much faith did Lazarus have that Yeshua would raise him? Lazarus had no faith; he was dead!" Yet the Scriptures record what happened.

> Then Jesus, again groaning in Himself, came to the tomb. It was a cave, and a stone lay against it. Jesus said, "Take away the stone."
> Martha, the sister of him who was dead, said to Him, "Lord, by this time there is a stench, for he has been dead four days."

Jesus said to her, "Did I not say to you that if you would believe you would see the glory of G-D?" Then they took away the stone from the place where the dead man was lying. And Jesus lifted up His eyes and said, "Father, I thank You that You have heard Me. And I know that You always hear Me, but because of the people who are standing by I said this, that they may believe that You sent Me." Now when He had said these things, He cried with a loud voice, "Lazarus, come forth!" And he who had died came out bound hand and foot with graveclothes, and his face was wrapped with a cloth. Jesus said to them, "Loose him, and let him go."

—JOHN 11:38–44, NKJV

Our heavenly Father, YHWH, has the ability to lift even the dead from the grave and bring back hope and faith where there was none.

LORD, You have brought up my soul from Sheol; You have kept me alive, that I would not go down to the pit.

—PSALM 30:3, NASB

King David alluded to YHWH lifting his soul from the pits of hell (the most horrible state he had ever faced as a result of his sin of adultery with Bathsheba and the murder of her husband). The hand of YHWH kept him alive and protected and rescued him from disgrace and being vanquished. In fact, in the New Testament, in Acts 13:22 (NIV), it is written about David:

I have found *David* son of Jesse, *a man after my own heart*; he will do everything I want him to do.

May we declare as King David declared in Psalm 30:1 (NKJV):

I will extol You, O [YHWH], for You have lifted me up, and have not let my foes rejoice over me.

PRAYER OF DECLARATION

Heavenly Father, I rejoice in Your being near me, even when I had no cognizance of Your presence. Your strong hand of salvation is always available to me. All I need to do is humble myself and turn toward You.

Your Word says, "But You, O [YHWH], are a shield for me, my glory and the One who lifts up my head" (Ps. 3:3, NKJV). I confess that there is no one like You. As King David wrote in the psalms, I join him in this declaration: "And now my head shall be lifted up above my enemies all around me; therefore I will offer sacrifices of joy in His tabernacle; I will sing, yes, I will sing praises to [YHWH]" (Ps. 27:6, NKJV).

THE HEBREW WORD FOR *COUNTENANCE*

The LORD lift His countenance upon you.
—NUMBERS 6:26

THE HEBREW WORD for *countenance*, again, is *panim*, which we have already discussed on Day 14 about the word *face*. This word is plural because it describes the entire behavioral actions of a person. It means everything that makes up who you are.

King David wrote of the power of having the "countenance of G-D upon us."

> There are many who say, "Who will show us any good?" [YHWH], lift up the light of Your countenance upon us.
> —PSALM 4:6, NKJV

Our heavenly Father has lifted us in His divine, strong, and loving arms, and He carries us. Yet now, like the loving Father He is, we look up at His face as He smiles on us and hugs us and even lovingly kisses us on our foreheads.

There are those who translate this portion differently based on the Hebrew translation. Instead of "The Lord lift His countenance upon you," they interpret it as "The Lord turn His countenance toward you."

The implication of this is that YHWH is turning His face toward you in order to take action on your behalf. YHWH is taking note of your situation, and He is ready to act on your behalf. The truth is that this portion of the Priestly Prayer indicates that the Father is never distant from us. We may have grown apart from Him, but He is never far from us.

> Behold, the eye of the LORD is on those who fear him, on those who
> hope in his steadfast love.
>
> —PSALM 33:18, ESV

There is no greater passage of Scripture that captures our heavenly
Father turning toward us, once we recognize Him, than that which
is found in the story of the prodigal son. The father of the prodigal
son didn't wait to rescue his son; instead, he ran toward his son and
embraced him.

> And he arose and came to his father. But when he was still a great
> way off, his father saw him and had compassion, and ran and fell on
> his neck and kissed him. And the son said to him, "Father, I have
> sinned against heaven and in your sight, and am no longer worthy to
> be called your son."
>
> But the father said to his servants, "Bring out the best robe and
> put it on him, and put a ring on his hand and sandals on his feet.
> And bring the fatted calf here and kill it, and let us eat and be merry;
> for this my son was dead and is alive again; he was lost and is found."
> And they began to be merry.
>
> —LUKE 15:20–24, NKJV

In this portion of the Priestly Prayer, YHWH turns His countenance toward us with the intent to minister to our needs.

SEE IT IN YOUR MIND'S EYE

YHWH blesses you...

In the first portion of the Priestly Prayer of the Blessing, your heavenly Father kneels in front of you, His spiritual son or daughter, as a
good parent desiring to make Himself available and minister to you.

YHWH keeps you...

In the second portion, your heavenly Father places His arms around you with a divine embrace, holding you in His strong arms of protection and security.

YHWH makes His face to shine upon you...

In this portion of the Priestly Prayer of the Blessing, it's as if He loosens His divine embrace, and while still keeping His holy hands on your shoulders, He pulls away enough for you to see Him face to face. You begin to experience His reality and His very person. Your heavenly Father makes His face to shine on you! This is G-D the Father saying to you, "You are My beloved son or daughter, in whom I am well pleased."

YHWH lifts His countenance upon you...

+ Your heavenly Father lifts you with His divine, strong arms and carries you, continually looking down at you as He walks. He is your loving heavenly Father.
+ He is also lifting all of who He is toward you. He is putting all of Himself at your disposal. He is bringing everything that He is to your aid.
+ He is supporting you with His entire being. Nothing is being withheld. You have the one true G-D of the universe on your side!
+ He is lifting His gaze continually toward you. Even when you aren't thinking about Him, He is near you and watches over you.
+ Your heavenly Father is giving you His full attention moment by moment every day.

The Scriptures speak of your heavenly Father desiring to make Himself fully available to you.

[YHWH] has made from one blood [Adam] every nation of men to live on the entire face of the earth, having appointed fixed times and the boundaries of their habitation, that they should seek [YHWH] so perhaps they might reach for Him and find Him, though He is not far from each one of us. "For in Him we live and move and have our being." As some of your own poets have said, "We are His offspring."

—ACTS 17:26–28

Through Messiah Yeshua both Jews and Gentiles have been given access to YHWH.

And [Yeshua, Jesus] came and preached peace to you who were far away and peace to those who were near. For through [Yeshua, Jesus] we both have access by one Spirit to [YHWH].

—EPHESIANS 2:17–18

Through Yeshua we have been born again as spiritual sons and daughters of the Most High G-D.

And because you are sons, [YHWH] has sent forth into our hearts the Spirit of His Son [Yeshua], crying, "Abba, Father!" Therefore you are no longer a servant, but a son, and if a son, then an heir of [YHWH] through [the Messiah].

—GALATIANS 4:6–7

Even if you are an orphan, YHWH desires to take care of you as your heavenly Father.

If my father and my mother forsake me, then the LORD will take me in.

—PSALM 27:10

PRAYER OF DECLARATION

Heavenly Father, I ask for forgiveness for the times I drifted apart from You. I repent for being so self-absorbed that I didn't recognize Your nearness to me. You are always watching me and ready to rescue me. Thank You that through this portion of the Priestly Prayer of the Blessing I am reminded that You are turning Your face toward me, ready to answer the cries of my heart. I pray in the name of Yeshua (Jesus) that You will send Your Ruach HaKodesh (Holy Spirit) to remind me that You are with me moment by moment every day.

YHWH IS AVAILABLE TO YOU

*Be strong and of a good courage. Fear not, nor be afraid of them, for
the LORD your [G-D], it is He who goes with you. He will not fail you,
nor forsake you.*

—DEUTERONOMY 31:6

T HE SCRIPTURES ARE clear that your heavenly Father is available
to you and wants the best for you.

He loves you like no other can love you!

> The LORD has appeared to him from afar, saying: "Indeed, I have
> loved you with an everlasting love; therefore with lovingkindness I
> have drawn you."
>
> —JEREMIAH 31:3

> Consider how much love the Father has given to us, that we should
> be called children of [G-D]. Therefore the world does not know us,
> because it did not know Him.
>
> —1 JOHN 3:1

He has compassion on you as a good Father!

> Like a father shows compassion to his children, so the LORD gives
> compassion to those who fear Him.
>
> —PSALM 103:13

> Blessed be [G-D], the Father of our Lord [Adonai] Jesus Christ
> [Yeshua the Messiah], the Father of mercies, and the [G-D] of all
> comfort.
>
> —2 CORINTHIANS 1:3

He cares for you even when others may forsake you!

Humble yourselves under the mighty hand of [G-D], that He may exalt you in due time. Cast all your care upon Him, because He cares for you.

—1 Peter 5:6–7

He delights in you and takes pleasure in His relationship with you!

For the Lord takes pleasure in His people; He will beautify the meek with salvation.

—Psalm 149:4

The Lord your [G-D] is in your midst, a Mighty One, who will save. He will rejoice over you with gladness, He will renew you with His love, He will rejoice over you with singing.

—Zephaniah 3:17

He desires intimacy with you and to call you by name!

But now, thus says the Lord who created you, O Jacob, and He who formed you, O Israel: Do not fear, for I have redeemed you; I have called you by your name; you are Mine. When you pass through waters, I will be with you. And through the rivers, they shall not overflow you. When you walk through the fire, you shall not be burned, nor shall the flame kindle on you.

—Isaiah 43:1–2

He gives you continual consideration!

The eyes of the Lord are on the righteous, and His ears are open to their cry.

—Psalm 34:15

He calls you His beloved friend!

The Scripture was fulfilled which says, "Abraham believed [G-D], and it was reckoned to him as righteousness," and he was called the friend of [G-D].

—James 2:23

He raises you even when you are forsaken by your flesh-and-blood parents and brethren!

> If my father and my mother forsake me, then the Lord will take me in.
>
> —Psalm 27:10

He desires to be patient and gentle with You!

> The Lord is merciful and gracious, slow to anger, and abounding in mercy.
>
> —Psalm 103:8

> The Lord is not slow concerning His promise, as some count slowness. But He is patient with us, because He does not want any to perish, but all to come to repentance.
>
> —2 Peter 3:9

He desires to teach and guide you throughout your life!

> I will instruct you and teach you in the way you should go; I will counsel you with my eye on you.
>
> —Psalm 32:8

> Thus says the Lord, your Redeemer, the Holy One of Israel: I am the Lord your [G-D], who teaches you to profit, who leads you in the way you should go.
>
> —Isaiah 48:17

He encourages and upholds you!

> Do not fear, for I am with you; do not be dismayed, for I am your [G-D]. I will strengthen you, I will help you, yes, I will uphold you with My righteous right hand.
>
> —Isaiah 41:10

He provides for you in ways you may never truly recognize!

The LORD is my shepherd; I shall not want.

—PSALM 23:1

Oh, fear the LORD, you His saints; for the ones who fear Him will not be in need.

—PSALM 34:9

He enjoys bestowing on you good gifts!

Every good gift and every perfect gift is from above and comes down from the Father of lights, with whom is no change or shadow of turning.

—JAMES 1:17

He is kindhearted and forgiving toward you!

For You, Lord, are good, and forgiving, abounding in kindness to all who call on You.

—PSALM 86:5

Who is a [G-D] like You, bearing iniquity and passing over transgression for the remnant of His inheritance? He does not remain angry forever, because He delights in benevolence. He will again have compassion upon us. He will tread down our iniquities, and cast all of our sins into the depths of the sea.

—MICAH 7:18–19

He disciplines you as a good Father who loves you and desires that you walk in His blessings and promises!

My son, do not despise the chastening of the LORD, nor be weary of His correction; for whom the LORD loves He corrects, even as a father the son in whom he delights.

—PROVERBS 3:11–12

PRAYER OF DECLARATION

Heavenly Father, I thank You for making Yourself available to me. You care for me like no other can with a selfless love. Your love is everlasting. Your compassion never fails me. I cast all my burdens and cares upon You. I know it is Your desire to keep all Your promises to me. I praise and worship You, Father, and I know You rejoice over me with gladness. Your ears are continually open to listen to my voice and my supplications. You are slow to anger, and You overflow with mercy.

I will listen for Your voice and look forward to Your instruction. I am comforted that Your eyes remain upon me continually, and as a good Father, You guide me, helping me stay on the narrow road of holiness. I rejoice in You and reverence Your holy name.

YHWH IS A PERFECT FATHER

I will be a Father to you, and you shall be My sons and daughters, says the Lord Almighty.

—2 Corinthians 6:18

In this portion of the Priestly Prayer of the Blessing, "The Lord lift His countenance upon you," the word *countenance* communicates the expression we behold on the face of YHWH. When we look into His loving eyes and behold His radiant face, we quickly sense that He is a perfect father.

Many of us grew up with imperfect parents. This sometimes taints our view of fatherhood. Yet the Creator of the family is YHWH, who created a man and a woman to marry.

> Therefore a man will leave his father and his mother and be joined to his wife, and they will become one flesh.
>
> —Genesis 2:24

YHWH created Adam and Eve to procreate and be parents.

> So [G-D] created man in His *own* image; in the image of [G-D] He created him; male and female He created them. [G-D] blessed them and said to them, "Be fruitful and multiply, and replenish the earth and subdue it. Rule over the fish of the sea and over the birds of the air and over every living thing that moves on the earth."
>
> —Genesis 1:27–28

It is YHWH who is our heavenly Father who demonstrates what it is to be a perfect father. His countenance reflects His qualities as the perfect Father.

Perfect love

Through words—Just as our natural parents can express their love to their children through the words of kindness, praise, and appreciation, so too YHWH has given us His Word made alive in us as He speaks it over us.

Through affection—YHWH also created us with a need to receive physical affection. Through this divine prayer of blessing, He makes Himself available so that we can experientially sense His divine love and embrace!

Through meaningful time spent together—In the natural the father or mother who takes time to listen to, play with, or just be with their children communicates that their children are important, worth their time and attention. YHWH makes Himself available to us through His divine prayer as He carries us in His arms and imparts the fullness of Himself, His love, and His pleasure concerning us!

Security

Every child needs to know the world into which they were born is a safe place to live! They need to know that their parents are there to protect them from harm! YHWH provides the utmost in security to us, His children!

Significance and purpose

Every person needs to know that their life has a purpose and value. Not only does YHWH unveil to us His calling, His purpose, and His destiny for our lives while here on earth, but He also enables us to accomplish it.

The promise of YHWH to us is:

> I will be a Father to you, and you shall be My sons and daughters, says the Lord Almighty.

—2 Corinthians 6:18

In our English Bibles this portion of the Priestly Prayer of the Blessing is:

The LORD lift His countenance upon you…

—NUMBERS 6:26

The amplified Hebrew-to-English translation of this portion is:

May YHWH (YeHoVaH, YaHWeH, your heavenly Father) lift up and carry His fullness of being toward you (bringing everything that He has to your aid), supporting you with His divine embrace and His entire being.

PRAYER OF DECLARATION

Heavenly Father, I confess my love for You and my appreciation that You are the perfect Father. I receive Your perfect love. Your words of wisdom and encouragement keep me centered on fulfilling Your destiny and calling for my life. I thank You for all the good things I am able to accomplish. I praise You for Your continued protection and security. I pray in the name of Yeshua (Jesus) that You will continue to unveil deeper revelations and glimpses of my future to help me in my pursuit to help others turn to You and enter Your kingdom.

MAY YHWH GIVE YOU PEACE

THE HEBREW WORD FOR *GIVE*

The LORD lift His countenance upon you,
and give you peace.

—NUMBERS 6:26

THUS FAR ON our thirty-day journey, we have dealt with YHWH making Himself available to us so He can impart the greatest gift we could ever receive—having His name placed on us. I am referring to His very person, His holy character, and His power and authority being imparted to us. This final portion of the divine prayer of blessing deals with what He desires to give us through His appearance and divine embrace.

The next-to-the-last word in the Priestly Prayer of the Blessing is *give*. The Hebrew word for *give* is *siym*, which has other meanings: "to put, place, set, appoint, make...lay, put or lay upon, lay (violent) hands on...direct toward, to extend (compassion)...ordain, establish, found, appoint, constitute, make, determine, fix...station...plant... transform into...fashion, work, bring to pass...make for a sign."[1]

Today let's contemplate the many things that YHWH (our heavenly Father) gives us.

1. His breath of life

Job 33:4 says, "The Spirit of [G-D] has made me, and the breath of the Almighty has given me life." YHWH (your heavenly Father) is constantly breathing, inhaling, and exhaling, as we also do.

According to an article in the *Daily Mail* by Claire Bates, scientists have discovered that a couple's breathing patterns and heart rates would sync after sitting close to each other. "They didn't even have to be holding hands or talking for this to happen."[2]

As we get closer to our heavenly Father, our breathing will become affected by His. When He exhales, we inhale to receive more of His very breath spiritually so we can be filled with more of His person, His holy character, and His power and authority.

Three days after Yeshua (Jesus) died on Passover, on the Feast of Firstfruits, He appeared as the resurrected One before His disciples. He then imparted the nature of G-D (the fruit of the Spirit) through imparting the Holy Spirit within them by breathing on them. (See John 20:21–22.)

2. Wealth and prosperity

> But you must remember the LORD your [G-D], for it is He who gives you the ability to get wealth, so that He may establish His covenant which He swore to your fathers, as it is today.
>
> —DEUTERONOMY 8:18

Yeshua clarified that it was the Father's heart for us to walk in abundance! "The thief does not come, except to steal and kill and destroy. I came that they may have life, and that they may have it more abundantly" (John 10:10).

YHWH (our heavenly Father) gives us all we need to accomplish our G-D-given destiny and purpose! Paul wrote to Timothy, "Command those who are rich in this world that they not be conceited, nor trust in uncertain riches, but in the living [G-D], who richly gives us all things to enjoy" (1 Tim. 6:17).

3. Rest and safety from your enemies

Deuteronomy 12:10 reminds us, "He gives you rest from all your enemies round about, so that you dwell in safety."

Yeshua tells us that we shouldn't strive, but rather enter His light and easy yoke: "Take My yoke upon you, and learn from Me. For I am meek and lowly in heart, and you will find rest for your souls. For My yoke is easy, and My burden is light" (Matt. 11:29–30).

4. Strength and power

Psalm 68:35 says, "O [G-D], You are awesome from Your sanctuaries; the [G-D] of Israel is He who gives strength and power to people. Blessed be [G-D]!"

5. Rain for harvest

In Jeremiah 5:24 we read, "They do not say in their heart, 'Let us now fear the LORD our [G-D], who gives rain, both the former and the latter, in its season. He reserves for us the appointed weeks of the harvest.'"

6. Wisdom, knowledge, and joy

Solomon wrote in Ecclesiastes 2:26, "For to a man who is pleasing before Him, [G-D] gives wisdom, knowledge, and joy; but to the sinner He gives the work of gathering and collecting to give him who is pleasing before [G-D]. Also this is vanity and chasing the wind."

7. Unmerited favor

James' epistle tells us, "He gives more grace. For this reason it says: '[G-D] resists the proud, but gives grace to the humble'" (Jas. 4:6).

But the greatest thing that your heavenly Father wants to give you is His peace. The Hebrew word is *shalom*, which means so much more than it does in English. Before I can give you the amplified Hebrew-to-English translation of this final portion, tomorrow we must dig deeper into the meaning of the Hebrew word for *give*.

PRAYER OF DECLARATION

Heavenly Father, thank You for this deeper revelation of Your Priestly Prayer of the Blessing. I am overwhelmed with Your desire to give Your spiritual sons and daughters good things. I thank You for giving me the breath of life and that when I walk in synchronization with You in my spirit, You fill me with more of Your very person, Your holy character, and Your power and authority. I thank You for Your daily provision, giving me what I need to accomplish Your daily assignments and calling for my life. I thank You for giving me rest and a safe dwelling place from my enemies.

Thank You for Your impartation of strength and power. I am grateful that You extend to me Your wisdom, knowledge, and fullness of joy. I recommit to a life of pursuing intimacy with You, heavenly Father, as well as with Yeshua (Jesus) and Your Ruach HaKodesh (Holy Spirit).

EXPLORING MORE ABOUT GIVING

You will be enriched in every way so that you can always be generous. And when we take your gifts to those who need them, they will thank [G-D].

—2 CORINTHIANS 9:11, NLT

IN THIS PORTION of the Priestly Prayer, "And give you peace," I'd like to explore in a deeper way the importance of giving: *siym*.

It is YHWH (our heavenly Father) who demonstrates how willing He is to give His spiritual sons and daughters good things. The Scriptures are clear that our G-D is an extravagant giver. In John 10:10 (NLT), Yeshua (Jesus) said:

The thief's purpose is to steal and kill and destroy. My purpose is to give them a rich and satisfying [*abundant*] life.

When Yeshua said this, He was speaking on behalf of the heavenly Father. The greatest thing that YHWH has given us is eternal salvation.

For G-D [the heavenly Father] so loved the world that He gave His only begotten Son, that whoever believes in Him [Yeshua] should not perish but have everlasting life.

—JOHN 3:16, NKJV

Yet we understand from *The Priestly Prayer of the Blessing* that it is the Father's desire to make Himself available to us and demonstrate the value of being extravagant givers.

Give, and it will be given to you: good measure, pressed down, shaken together, and running over will be put into your bosom. For with the same measure that you use, it will be measured back to you.

—LUKE 6:38, NKJV

We are created in the likeness of G-D the Father. No matter how much we give, we cannot outgive G-D. There is a principle within G-D's kingdom that when we give, we receive back far more. This may be in the area of our finances, or it may be experiencing the abundance of YHWH in other areas of our lives, such as relationships, health, miracles, breakthroughs, and more!

> But this I say: He who sows sparingly will also reap sparingly, and he who sows bountifully will also reap bountifully.
>
> —2 CORINTHIANS 9:6, NKJV

We often think of that verse concerning giving our tithes and offerings. But we can give (or sow) into the lives of others using our time, treasure, and talents.

> Charge them that are rich in this world, that they be not high-minded, nor trust in uncertain riches, but in the living [G-D], who giveth us richly all things to enjoy; that they do good, that they be rich in good works, ready to distribute, willing to communicate; laying up in store for themselves a good foundation against the time to come, that they may lay hold on eternal life.
>
> —1 TIMOTHY 6:17–19, KJV

We who have received much from the goodness of YHWH are encouraged to sow good things into the lives of others, and by doing so, we store up our rewards in heaven where even greater eternal gifts will be available for us for all eternity.

> Do not be deceived, G-D is not mocked; for whatever a man sows, that he will also reap. For he who sows to his flesh will of the flesh reap corruption, but he who sows to the Spirit will of the Spirit reap everlasting life. And let us not grow weary while doing good, for in due season we shall reap if we do not lose heart. Therefore, as we

have opportunity, let us do good to all, especially to those who are of the household of faith.

—Galatians 6:7–10, nkjv

Those verses deal with the kingdom law of sowing (giving) and reaping. YHWH encourages us to sow into the Spirit, rather than our flesh. We should consider this in the three different areas of giving:

1. Time—What do we do with the time YHWH has given each day? Are we doing things that sow into the Spirit? Are we worshipping, praying, reading, and meditating on the Word of G-D? Investing our time in the name of Yeshua (Jesus) to encourage others helps them realize how good the heavenly Father has been to us.

2. Treasure—Are we hoarding what we have received as gifts from the Lord, whether it be finances, good relationships, or provision of food, clothing, or living accommodations? Are we sowing into the lives of others who are in need?

3. Talents—Are we using the gifts given to us by YHWH and investing them to minister to others? Are we committed to using them to reach souls for the kingdom of G-D?

Do not lay up for yourselves treasures on earth, where moth and rust destroy and where thieves break in and steal; but lay up for yourselves treasures in heaven, where neither moth nor rust destroys and where thieves do not break in and steal. For where your treasure is, there your heart will be also.

—Matthew 6:19–21, nkjv

In this portion of the Priestly Prayer of the Blessing it's important to recognize that every good thing given to us from our heavenly

Father is given with the expectation that it will be used to touch the lives of others and help usher them into a relationship with Him.

Prayer of Declaration

Heavenly Father, I ask for forgiveness for the times I didn't credit You with the good things I have received in my life. Anything good that has happened in my life was set up, appointed, established, or provided directly by You. I give You all the glory and praise! I ask for forgiveness for the times I hoarded what You so graciously provided to me. I thank You especially for the gift of the Ruach HaKodesh (Holy Spirit) within me. I ask in the name of Yeshua (Jesus) that You help me be gracious in giving of my time, treasure, and talents to minister to the needs of others You have placed in my life.

THE HEBREW WORD FOR *PEACE*

The LORD bless you and keep you; the LORD make His face to shine upon you, and be gracious unto you; the LORD lift His countenance upon you, and give you peace.

—NUMBERS 6:24–26

THIS FINAL WORD in G-D's divine prayer of the blessing is abstract in English and Greek. We tend to think of the word *peace* as meaning the absence of strife and war, but it is so much more! The root word is *shalam*, which means to make amends. This is emphasized in Scripture.

> The owner of the pit must make restitution. He must give money to their owner, and the dead animal will be his.
>
> —EXODUS 21:34

One of the meanings of *shalom* is to make restitution, but its main meaning is to make something even better than its former or original state. When we have shalom, promises and blessings that were robbed from us by the enemy of our souls are restored when our heavenly Father imparts His restorative powers to us. He restores us to a right relationship with Him through the gift of forgiveness and justification. He can restore our earthly relationships.

He can even restore days and years that have been lost to the effects of sin. (See Joel 2:25.) That has to be the greatest evidence of the extravagant nature of G-D's mercy. Not only can He renew your life and redeem your future, but YHWH can also redeem your past.

The heavenly Father restores sight to the blind, the ability to walk to the crippled, hearing to the deaf, and new, clean skin to the diseased. (See Mark 8:22–26; Matthew 9:2–8; Mark 7:31–37; Luke

5:12–25.) G-D doesn't just heal a condition; He restores life, security, and hope to the brokenhearted!

G-D Makes All Things New

When the Priestly Prayer of the Blessing is pronounced over us, shalom enables us to make up for lost time, bestows new identities, and creates new life! YHWH (our heavenly Father) promises good plans for His people, plans that include a hopeful future!

> For I know the plans that I have for you, says [YHWH], plans for peace and not for evil, to give you a future and a hope.
>
> —Jeremiah 29:11

The ultimate peace (shalom) will be when YHWH ushers in His kingdom of heaven onto the earth.

> And [G-D] will wipe away every tear from their eyes; there shall be no more death, nor sorrow, nor crying. There shall be no more pain, for the former things have passed away.
>
> —Revelation 21:4, nkjv

There will be no sickness, pain, sorrow, or crying because the joy of the Lord will fill the earth as the perfect peace of YHWH (the heavenly Father) abides on the planet.

Our Daily Hope

Yeshua taught us how to pray for shalom (perfect peace as it is in heaven). The prayer is often referred to as the Lord's Prayer.

> Therefore pray in this manner: Our Father who is in heaven, hallowed be Your name.
>
> —Matthew 6:9

Yeshua is referring to G-D's sacred name: YHWH (YeHoVaH, YaHWeH).

Your kingdom come; Your will be done on earth, as it is in heaven.
                                                    —MATTHEW 6:10

In heaven there is perfect shalom. Through the divine prayer of the
Priestly Prayer of the Blessing, you can begin to tap into a portion of
heaven coming into your life now! In the very presence of the Father
you receive what the Father has!

He brings with Him heaven's atmosphere. Heaven has no limita-
tion, sickness, oppression, depression, or emotional upheaval. It has
no warfare, lack, condemnation, murder, theft, conniving, assault and
battery, or injustice! Heaven only has perfect shalom: fulfillment and
wellness of being, prosperity, provision, love, joy, and perfection! True
shalom is to have every part of your life brought back to completeness
and wholeness!

PRAYER OF DECLARATION

*Heavenly Father, I thank You and praise You for Your Priestly
Prayer of the Blessing. You have made me aware of how much
You truly love me. Thank You for the greatest gift of all, Your
shalom. Now I understand the completeness and wholeness I shall
receive each day from You through this portion of the prayer are
allowing me to experience Your kingdom of heaven alive in me.*

*When Yeshua (Jesus), Your only begotten Son, was asked by
His disciples how to pray, He taught them, "Our Father who is in
heaven, hallowed be Your name. Your kingdom come; Your will
be done on earth, as it is in heaven." I now understand through
this Priestly Prayer that it's as if I can pray, "Your Kingdom come
in me. Let Your will be done in me as it is in heaven!"*

*I am filled with anticipation, as I am now ready to begin pro-
nouncing the Amplified Hebrew-to-English version of Your divine
prayer over myself in the name (shem) of Yeshua (Jesus). I realize
that as I pray this prayer in Yeshua's name, I am pronouncing it*

in the person of Yeshua, with His holy character and with His power and authority. Yeshua is seated in the holy of holies at Your right hand, heavenly Father. It is Yeshua (Jesus) praying it through my lips as my High Priest.

I look forward to You, heavenly Father, placing Your name (shem) upon me every day.

BRINGING SHALOM TO EARTH

For unto us a child is born, unto us a son is given, and the government shall be upon his shoulder. And his name shall be called Wonderful Counselor, Mighty [G-D], Eternal Father, Prince of Peace.

—ISAIAH 9:6

YESTERDAY WE LEARNED that true peace (shalom) exists in the dwelling place of YHWH in heaven, which includes completeness and wholeness. This is reinforced when a Jewish person says, "Shabbat shalom," after a long week of working and feeling drained and tired. He is saying, "May the G-D of Israel restore you this Sabbath and bring about wholeness and completeness for you."

Today we will explore how this peace of G-D's dwelling place in heaven has been brought to us on earth. Yeshua was prophesied to be the Sar Shalom—in English, the Prince of Peace—which perfectly describes our Messiah's ministry and personality.

In Luke chapter 2 we read that the night Yeshua was born as the Sar Shalom—the Prince of Peace—YHWH (the heavenly Father) appeared, along with the angel of the Lord, in the form of the Shekinah glory. Some biblical scholars believe these weren't average shepherds but Israelites who belonged to the tribe of the Levites (the priests) and were tending the sheep to be used as sacrificial animals for the holy temple observances.

Many theologians believe that the angel of the Lord in Luke 2 was part of a theophany—an appearance of G-D the Father Himself. The Shekinah glory of YHWH accompanied the angel of the Lord. Just as the priests were overcome and couldn't minister in the tabernacle and holy temple when the glory came, so too the shepherds in the field were overcome by G-D's Shekinah glory.

The Sar Shalom, the promised Prince of Peace, Yeshua the Messiah, was born. It will be He who, in His second coming, ushers in the Messianic Millennial Age, when New Jerusalem descends from heaven and the glory of YHWH (our heavenly Father) fills the earth, bringing the atmosphere of heaven on the earth.

When "Ultimate Shalom" Invades Earth

Shalom is an all-encompassing word for the good that comes from YHWH when He and Yeshua come to earth as New Jerusalem descends from heaven, ushering in the Messianic Age.[1]

Ultimate shalom will become tangible when the very atmosphere of heaven itself invades the earth. The Scriptures declare that all creation groans for this.

> We know that the whole creation groans and travails in pain together until now. Not only that, but we also, who have the first fruits of the Spirit, groan within ourselves while eagerly waiting for the adoption, the redemption of our bodies.
>
> —Romans 8:22–23

During the Messianic Millennial Age, the earth's atmosphere and humanity's very nature will be docile. (See Micah 4:3.) During the Messianic Millennial Age, there will be such an atmosphere of shalom on the earth that predatory animals will become tame and will no longer eat flesh but rather graze on grass. (See Isaiah 11:6–10.)

The Garden of Eden was heaven on the earth. I believe that through G-D's divine prayer, we can begin to experience a return to Eden. In *Strong's Concordance* we see that shalom encompasses many different areas of our lives.

Shalom means completeness, wholeness, health, peace, welfare, safety, soundness, tranquility, prosperity, perfectness, fullness, rest, harmony, the absence of agitation or discord. Shalom comes from the root verb *shalom* meaning to be complete, perfect and full. In modern Hebrew the related word *Shelem* means to pay for, and *Shulam* means to be fully paid.[2]

In our English Bibles this portion of the Priestly Prayer of the Blessing is:

…and give you peace.

—Numbers 6:26

The amplified Hebrew-to-English translation of this portion is:

May YHWH (YeHoVaH, YaHWeH, your heavenly Father) set in place all you need to be whole and complete so you can walk in victory, moment by moment, by the power of the Holy Spirit. May He give you supernatural health, peace, welfare, safety, soundness, tranquility, prosperity, perfection, fullness, rest, and harmony, as well as the absence of agitation and discord.

Prayer of Declaration

Heavenly Father, I thank You that Yeshua (Jesus), Your only begotten Son, is my Sar Shalom, the Prince of Peace. I know that it will be Yeshua who ushers in the Messianic Millennial Age, as He and You, heavenly Father, descend and bring the atmosphere of heaven onto the earth. This will be the ultimate shalom.

Through Your Priestly Prayer of the Blessing, You are allowing me to begin experiencing a taste of what it will be like during the fullness of Your reign with Yeshua, Your Son. I am ready to receive Your shalom, Your completeness and wholeness, supernatural health, peace, welfare, safety, soundness of mind, and so much more!

I declare that I will be pronouncing the amplified Hebrew-to-English version of Your Priestly Prayer of the Blessing every day over myself and others as I am able. I look forward to journaling the deepening of my relationship with You, heavenly Father, as I experience a supernatural, intimate, and experiential relationship with You in a way I have never had before!

PRAYING THE PRIESTLY PRAYER

THE AMPLIFIED HEBREW-TO-ENGLISH TRANSLATION

But each day the LORD pours his unfailing love upon me,
and through each night I sing his songs, praying to [G-D]
who gives me life.

—Psalm 42:8, NLT

GET READY TO receive the Priestly Prayer of the Blessing pronounced over you! Remember, the actual name (*shem*)—that of YHWH (your heavenly Father)—is being placed on you through the Priestly Prayer of the Blessing. Throughout the previous sections of this book, I walked you through all the abstract English words of this prayer, revealing the original Hebrew language's deeper meaning. Today it is time to put it all together.

After you have proclaimed the prayer over yourself, you can also listen to the prayer being proclaimed by me in the amplified Hebrew-to-English translation and then sung over you in Hebrew by the world-renowned Messianic worship leader Paul Wilbur. Simply type the URL www.WarrenMarcus.com/prayer into your internet browser to access this version of the prayer being sung in either audio or video form. Both formats have been provided as a way to bless you powerfully.

In our English Bibles the prayer is stated in the following way:

The LORD bless you and keep you; the LORD make His face to shine upon you, and be gracious unto you; the LORD lift His countenance upon you, and give you peace.

—Numbers 6:24–26

Now get ready to begin receiving a supernatural impartation of the Priestly Prayer of the Blessing as you proclaim it over yourself in Hebrew in the person of, the holy character of, and the power and authority of Yeshua, the Jewish High Priest in heaven! After you pronounce the amplified Hebrew-to-English translation over yourself, pray the following prayer and continue reading this chapter.

YHWH (Father G-D), I thank You that I can walk in Your shalom. You are the One who created the heavens and the earth. Every knee shall bow, and every tongue shall confess Your name and the name of Your Son. Father, I thank You. I receive now Your name placed on me, meaning Your person, Your character, Your authority, and Your supernatural power. Help me, YHWH, to demonstrate to others who You are so they too can experience Your reality. Amen.

יְבָרֶכְךָ יְהוָה וְיִשְׁמְרֶךָ:

The LORD bless you, and keep you;

יָאֵר יְהוָה פָּנָיו אֵלֶיךָ וִיחֻנֶּךָּ:

The LORD make His face shine on you, And be gracious to you;

יִשָּׂא יְהוָה פָּנָיו אֵלֶיךָ וְיָשֵׂם לְךָ שָׁלוֹם:

The LORD lift up His countenance on you, And give you peace.

In our English Bibles it reads:

The LORD bless you...

But in my amplified Hebrew-to-English translation of the prayer, it is:

May YHWH (YeHoVaH, YaHWeH, your heavenly Father) kneel before you (making Himself available to you as your heavenly Father) so He can grant or bestow upon you His promises and gifts.

In the first portion of the Priestly Prayer of the Blessing, YHWH kneels in front of you, His spiritual son or daughter, as a good parent desiring to make Himself available and minister to you. This requires a response. Do you keep standing, or do you humble yourself and kneel in front of Him?

In our English Bibles it reads:

The LORD bless you and keep you...

But in my amplified translation of the prayer, it is:

May YHWH (YeHoVaH, YaHWeH, your heavenly Father) guard you with a hedge of thorny protection that will prevent Satan and all your enemies from harming your body, soul, mind, and spirit, your loved ones, and all your possessions.

In this second portion your heavenly Father places His arms around you with a divine embrace, holding you in His strong arms of protection and security.

In our English Bibles it reads:

The LORD make His face to shine upon you...

But in my amplified Hebrew-to-English translation of the prayer, it is:

May YHWH (YeHoVaH, YaHWeH, your heavenly Father) illuminate the wholeness of His being toward you, continually bringing to you order, so that you will fulfill your G-D-given destiny and purpose.

In this portion of the Priestly Prayer of the Blessing, it's as if He loosens His divine embrace. While still keeping His holy hands on your shoulders, He pulls away enough for you to see Him face to face so you can begin to experience His reality and person.

In our English Bibles it reads:

And be gracious unto you...

But in my amplified translation it is:

May YHWH (YeHoVaH, YaHWeH, your heavenly Father) provide you with perfect love and fellowship, never leaving you, and give you sustenance, provision, and friendship.

Your heavenly Father reveals His perfect love to you as your perfect Daddy with loving eyes and a beatific smile. He looks past your weaknesses and your frailties, pledging that He will never leave you and that He will provide you with His love, fellowship, and friendship. He says, "You are My beloved son or daughter, in whom I am well pleased."

In our English Bibles it reads:

The LORD lift His countenance upon you...

But in my amplified Hebrew-to-English translation of the prayer, it is:

May YHWH (YeHoVaH, YaHWeH, your heavenly Father) lift up and carry His fullness of being toward you (bringing everything that

He has to your aid), supporting you with His divine embrace and His entire being.

This is your heavenly Father lifting you up with His divine, strong arms and carrying you, continually looking down at you as He walks. He is your loving heavenly Father.

He is also lifting all of who He is toward you. He is putting all of Himself at your disposal. He is bringing everything that He is to your aid. He is supporting you with His entire being. Nothing is being withheld. You have the one true G-D of the universe on your side!

~~~

In our English Bibles it reads:

And give you peace...

But in my amplified Hebrew-to-English translation, it is:

May YHWH (YeHoVaH, YaHWeH, your heavenly Father) set in place all you need to be whole and complete so you can walk in victory, moment by moment, by the power of the Holy Spirit. May He give you supernatural health, peace, welfare, safety, soundness, tranquility, prosperity, perfection, fullness, rest, and harmony, as well as the absence of agitation and discord.

HOW TO PRONOUNCE THE DIVINE PRAYER OVER YOURSELF AND OTHERS

I encourage you to pronounce this amazing prayer over yourself and others every day. To administer this divine prayer over others in the manner prescribed by YHWH, you must be sure that you are born-again. If you are not sure that you have been born again, you can say the following prayer as an example or simply pray (talk to G-D) in your own words that express what you feel in your heart.

I come to You, G-D of Israel, and humble myself before You. I repent of my sins (my rebellion) against You and now desire to embrace what You call holy. I accept the invitation of Yeshua to sync my life with His. According to His invitation, I accept Him as my Messiah, Lord, and High Priest by faith.

Next, Yeshua said, "Come to Me, all you who labor and are heavily burdened, and I will give you rest. Take My yoke upon you, and learn from Me. For I am meek and lowly in heart, and you will find rest for your souls. For My yoke is easy, and My burden is light" (Matt. 11:28–30). A yoke is a wooden crosspiece fastened over the necks of two animals. When Yeshua says we are to take His yoke upon us, He uses the term figuratively as an invitation to sync our lives to His. Now it's time to respond to His invitation with another prayer.

Yeshua (Jesus), I come to You, for I have been laboring, and I have been under a heavy burden! You promised that if I take Your yoke upon me that You will give me rest. Now I will walk alongside You and get to know You, for You are humble and meek. I will learn everything about You—what You taught, how You lived, and what the future holds for me. I will take counsel with Your written instructions (the Bible), and I look forward to when You return as King of kings! Your promise to me is eternal life and that walking with You will be easy and the burdens of this life will be light.

If you prayed that prayer or something similar from your heart, you have just become born-again! Welcome to the family of G-D! Now that you are truly born-again and have been made an adopted son or daughter of the one true G-D of Israel, you can effectively pronounce this prayer over yourself and others every day. Yeshua is your High Priest, and He wants to say the Priestly Prayer of the Blessing over you every day!

What You Are About to Do Is Supernatural!

As you speak out loud over yourself this amplified Hebrew-to-English translation of the Priestly Prayer of the Blessing, it will be your voice speaking, but by proxy it will be Yeshua Himself in heaven speaking it through your mouth.

Your ears will hear the prayer of blessing. Your mind will be washed and regenerated through this prayer. Supernaturally the name of the one true G-D of Israel, YHWH (YeHoVaH, YaHWeH, your heavenly Father), will be placed on you. To have His name (*shem*) placed on you means the one true G-D of Israel's very breath—the essence of who the bearer of the name truly is, His very person, His holy character, and His power and authority—will be imparted to you.

Now continue to pray this amplified Hebrew-to-English translation of the prayer out loud every day.

Prayer of Declaration

Here is the complete prayer in English, expanded with the Amplified Hebrew-to-English Translation of each phrase.

The Lord bless you...

> May YHWH (YeHoVaH, YaHWeH) kneel before you (making Himself available to you as your heavenly Father) so He can grant or bestow upon you His promises and gifts.

And keep you...

> May YHWH (YeHoVaH, YaHWeH, your heavenly Father) guard you with a hedge of thorny protection that will prevent Satan and all your enemies from harming your body, soul, mind, and spirit, your loved ones, and all your possessions.

The LORD make his face shine upon you...

May YHWH (YeHoVaH, YaHWeH, your heavenly Father) illuminate the wholeness of His being toward you, continually bringing to you order, so that you will fulfill your G-D-given destiny and purpose.

And be gracious to you...

May YHWH (YeHoVaH, YaHWeH, your heavenly Father) provide you with perfect love and fellowship, never leaving you, and give you sustenance, provision, and friendship.

The LORD lift his countenance on you...

May YHWH (YeHoVaH, YaHWeH, your heavenly Father) lift up and carry His fullness of being toward you (bringing everything that He has to your aid), supporting you with His divine embrace and His entire being.

And give you peace.

May YHWH (YeHoVaH, YaHWeH, your heavenly Father) set in place all you need to be whole and complete so you can walk in victory, moment by moment, by the power of the Holy Spirit. May He give you supernatural health, peace, welfare, safety, soundness, tranquility, prosperity, perfection, fullness, rest, and harmony, as well as the absence of agitation and discord.

WARREN M. MARCUS

WARREN HAS BEEN a Messianic Jewish believer since October 1974. He is ordained as a Spirit-filled evangelist in the Southern Baptist denomination. Today he serves as vice president of Sid Roth's Messianic Vision Inc., where he oversees the radio and television productions, including the weekly *It's Supernatural!* television show.

Warren has pastored a weekly One New Man (Creation) Meeting every Saturday at Steele Creek Church of Charlotte in North Carolina. His teaching of the Hebrew roots has helped many in the church today enter a deeper relationship with the G-D of Israel and Jesus the Messiah. You can contact him on his website at www.WarrenMarcus.com.

Warren has produced the Great North American Revival DVD series, which features his award-winning documentaries on the Toronto Blessing, the Smithton Outpouring, and the Brownsville Revival. While filming these documentaries, he was profoundly impacted, and he shares what he learned about these great moves of G-D. The series includes rare, anointed footage from these great revivals. People who have watched these videos have reported the glory of G-D invading their homes! You can view this revival series by going to www.WarrenMarcus.com/revival.

Warren is known for award-winning productions, including the Christian Broadcasting Network's animated children's Bible stories the Superbook series and *Flying House*. He also produced the highest-rated religious TV special of all time, *Don't Ask Me, Ask God*. It featured Hollywood stars such as Michael J. Fox, Ned Beatty, and others. This prime-time TV special garnered a 10.5 Nielsen TV rating with an audience of more than sixteen million people.